UNFORGETTABLE

A Tribute to 100 Icons Who Died Too Young

First published by Parragon in 2012
Parragon
Queen Street House
4 Queen Street
Bath BA1 1HE, UK
www.parragon.com

All photographs © Getty Images except those on pages 104, 105, 123, 124,
137, 155t © Corbis
Copyright © Parragon Books Ltd 2012

Produced by Atlantic Publishing

A catalogue record for this book is available from the British Library.

ISBN 978-1-4454-6616-3

Printed in China

UNFORGETTABLE

A Tribute to 100 Icons
Who Died Too Young

Tim Hill

PaRragon

Bath • New York • Singapore • Hong Kong • Cologne • Delhi
Melbourne • Amsterdam • Johannesburg • Auckland • Shenzhen

Contents

Introduction

At the dawn of the 20th century, the motor car was in its infancy, the skies had yet to be conquered by a heavier-than-air machine, the telephone and wireless telegraphy were cutting-edge communications technology. News from faraway lands was exotic and quixotic, its dissemination an unwieldy business. The last one hundred years has witnessed an information explosion. It is the era of mass communication, the televisual and cinematic age. It has been an epochal period in the political sphere, while sport and entertainment have become billion-dollar industries whose stars we place on vertiginous pedestals.

The global village has given us heroic figures with a global reach. Where stellar achievement leads, celebrity follows. We lionize those whose talents have taken them to the pinnacle of their field. But our idols are no less prone to the vicissitudes of life than the rest of us; they are equally susceptible to tragic accidents, to being in the wrong place at the wrong time, to being struck down by illness; and, on occasion, to contributing to their own downfall with dissolute ways.

Any untimely death is a tragedy, but when those esteemed by millions face their own mortality long before their time, mourning takes on a different hue. The public outpouring that attended the deaths of Rudolph Valentino, Elvis Presley, John Lennon, Diana, Princess of Wales and Michael Jackson made their departures extraordinary global events. On such occasions eulogy and grief become a grand-scale shared experience. Just as we were touched by their accomplishments and genius, so are we moved by their passing. The sense of loss is as universal as the acclaim. In many cases it goes beyond simple respect or homage; when those we revere leave the stage, vigils, shrines and pilgrimage often follow.

All of those profiled in these pages made their mark, leaving a rich, indelible legacy. Many, such as Marilyn Monroe, Freddie Mercury and Ayrton Senna, had reached the top of the tree, yet we still wonder how their lives and careers would have panned out had they lived. The Brazilian motor racing ace died doing what he loved best, what he did better than anybody, what thrilled his army of fans. Bruce McLaren and Dale Earnhardt Sr were out of the same mould, while Amy Johnson, Amelia Earhart and Steve Irwin also lost their lives doing what they excelled at, that brought so much pleasure to others.

James Dean also made it to the summit, but stood in that lofty position just long enough to make three memorable films before his date with destiny in a Porsche Spyder, his bedroom-poster looks frozen forever at 24 years of age. River Phoenix, Heath Ledger and Kurt Cobain were others who seemed scarcely to have etched their name into the public consciousness before they were gone. Their dazzling triumphs held out the promise of so much more that Fate decreed would never materialize. The same could be said of Bix Beiderbecke and Amy Winehouse; virtuosity and a self-destructive streak have all too often been opposite sides of the same coin. These pages are replete with personal histories of shooting stars that crashed and burned. Drug and alcohol abuse is a recurring theme. Judy Garland, John Belushi, Hank Williams and Charlie 'Bird' Parker are just some of those whose lives were blighted and truncated by drink and pills, but who brought inestimable joy to people's lives before they were terminally ravaged by their addictions.

Cobain and Winehouse are two members of the notorious '27 Club', whose number also includes Jimi Hendrix, Janis Joplin and Jim Morrison. The 1930s blonde bombshell Jean Harlow didn't even reach that age, carried off by a fatal illness at 26. Lou Gehrig, Bob Marley and Steve McQueen were similarly struck down, defeated in protracted battles, while sudden accidents befell the likes of Buddy Holly, Patsy Cline, Payne Stewart and Jeff Buckley. All of the above had their time in the spotlight, even if in some cases it was all too brief. For Anne Frank fame and acclaim came only after her demise, while the tortured, mentally fragile Nick Drake achieved cult status post-mortem with music largely disregarded during his short life.

Whether success arrived early or late, whether death was self-inflicted or as a result of tragic happenstance, we feel cheated of what might have been when our heroes are taken from us. Nowhere is this more keenly felt than in the political arena. With the assassinations of Martin Luther King, Robert Kennedy and Benazir Bhutto, hopes as well as lives were snuffed out. JFK and Winston Churchill died two years apart, but while we honoured the passing of a nonagenarian statesman, we grieved for what a 46-year-old president might have gone on to achieve.

This book charts the lives of one hundred luminaries from various fields who were snatched from us all too soon. Their extraordinary gifts put them on a different plane from the rest of us. They weren't superhuman, but they are immortalized by their achievements and in our hearts and memories.

Music Makers
Pop & Rock

Marc Bolan

HIGH PRIEST OF GLAM-ROCK
30 SEPTEMBER 1947 – 16 SEPTEMBER 1977

At the height of their popularity in the early 1970s, T Rex were selling 100,000 records a day. Androgynous frontman Marc Bolan was the driving force behind the 'Rexmania' phenomenon that swept the world.

London-born Mark Feld had poetic leanings from an early age. Once he picked up a guitar, music became his favoured medium of expression. Influenced by Dylan, he immersed himself in the folk scene, singing about wizards and satyrs. Myths and mysticism informed his writing. He performed briefly as Toby Tyler, before reinventing himself with a surname reportedly culled from his musical hero: Bob Dylan.

Despite the flowery conceits found in his lyrics, Bolan craved mainstream success. When that wasn't forthcoming with rock combo John's Children, he formed Tyrannosaurus Rex with percussionist Steve Took. Their psychedelic folk-rock sound found an audience and was there an album whose title and Tolkien-inspired artwork better reflected the zeitgeist than *My People Were Fair And Had Sky In Their Hair... But Now They're Content To Wear Stars On Their Brows?*

'I was and am a free spirit. I wanted to gather information and experience everything.'

Mickey Finn replaced Took, but the big change came in 1970, when Bolan rebranded the group T Rex and went electric, which Dylan himself had done. If Bolan alienated some of his old fans, as Dylan had done, he replaced them many times over as he became a teen idol. With 'Ride a White Swan', which reached No 2 in the United Kingdom, Bolan found a commercial groove repeated relentlessly over the next three years. 'Hot Love', 'Get It On', 'Jeepster', 'Telegram Sam' and 'Metal Guru' were all chart-toppers, part of a run of ten successive Top 5 hits. Decked out in glitter, make-up and flamboyant outfits, Bolan led the glam-rock charge, though America never quite got what all the fuss was about.

By 1975 the bubble had burst. The singles were scarcely raising a ripple. Bolan's alcohol and cocaine habit grew to serious proportions and the pretty-boy superstar piled on the pounds. He withdrew from the scene for a year and cleaned up his act, motivated in part by the birth of son Rolan by his girlfriend, former backing singer Gloria Jones.

Bolan's career enjoyed a revival with releases such as 'New York City' and 'I Love to Boogie', both Top 20 hits. He'd just fronted his own TV show shortly before his 30th birthday, when he was killed in a car accident. Gloria was driving them home after a night out in London when their Mini hit a tree.

Top: Marc Bolan with Gloria Jones, 1977.

Above: Elton John and Marc Bolan pictured at John Lennon's Tittenhurst Studio while filming Born to Boogie, *1972.*

Opposite: Bolan pictured in 1974.

Jeff Buckley

'A PURE DROP IN AN OCEAN OF NOISE'
17 NOVEMBER 1966 – 29 MAY 1997

'Grace is what matters, in anything ... it keeps you from reaching for the gun too quickly; it keeps you from destroying things too foolishly.' It was U2's Bono who described Jeff Buckley thus, a view shared by many other music legends, as well as a worldwide army of fans. It is all the more remarkable in that Buckley's reputation rests on a single studio album that barely raised a ripple on its initial release.

In his mid-teens, when he acquired a Gibson Les Paul, Jeff Buckley's avowed ambition was to become a guitar great. It would mark him out from his mother – a classically trained pianist – but, more importantly, circumvent comparisons with the father he scarcely knew. Tim Buckley, who split from Jeff's mother before he was born, was a revered figure on the musical landscape. Discovered while playing on the LA folk-club scene in the mid-1960s, he made nine albums over the next decade, effortlessly crossing genres. Tim didn't reap the commercial benefits that his talent merited; his influence grew after his death from an accidental overdose in 1975.

'I was captured by music at a really early age. It was the best thing in my life.'

After a long period of resistance, Jeff finally accepted himself as a vocalist. By 1990 he had made a demo that included embryonic versions of 'Last Goodbye' and 'Eternal Life', both of which would appear on his *Grace* album four years later. In 1991 he appeared in a tribute concert to his father in New York, prompting many to remark on an uncanny resemblance between the two, a likeness of bearing and mannerisms as well as looks. They also had in common extraordinary

Left: Jeff Buckley plays at the Glastonbury Festival, 1994.

Opposite: On stage in The Netherlands, 1995.

voices, each with a phenomenal range and a haunting, soulful quality.

Jeff had a dedicated following on the New York club circuit, and a four-track EP to his name, when Sony signed him to a three-album deal. The result was *Grace*, which featured work by Benjamin Britten, Leonard Cohen's 'Hallelujah' and a cover of 'Lilac Wine', plus a crop of originals. It was hailed a masterpiece. After the accompanying tour, Buckley's

thoughts turned to a new album. Expectations were high and there was a creative struggle, during which time he moved to Memphis. The material he wrote for the new work – already titled *My Sweetheart the Drunk* – had his band and studio bosses enraptured.

The songs were still in four-track demo form when Jeff Buckley drowned while taking a dip, fully clothed, in Wolf River. He was 30, two years older than Tim when he died.

Karen Carpenter

'VOICE OF THE HEART'
2 MARCH 1950 – 4 FEBRUARY 1983

The Carpenters bucked the 1970s trends in hard rock, glam-rock, disco and punk, their middle-of-the-road sound attracting an army of loyal fans. Richard Carpenter was the musical genius and master arranger, but it was his sister Karen's distinctive, hauntingly beautiful voice that carried a string of worldwide hits.

As kids growing up in New Haven, Connecticut, while Richard was mastering the piano, Karen was more likely to be found outside indulging in tomboyish pursuits. That changed somewhat after the family moved to Downey, California, in 1963, though when Karen took up the drums at high school, it was primarily to escape mathematics.

As a trio – with a tuba player on board – they won a Battle of the Bands contest in 1966 and came to RCA's attention. That deal soon foundered, the trio morphed into a group called Spectrum but eventually Richard and Karen decided to go it alone. Their breakthrough came when a demo tape landed on the desk of A & M co-founder Herb Alpert, who signed them in 1969.

The debut single, a slow-tempo version of The Beatles' 'Ticket to Ride', did moderate business. The follow-up was the Bacharach-David-penned 'Close to You', which gave them their first No 1 and a Grammy. Karen, happily ensconced behind her drum kit, was image-conscious and insecure, unwilling to take centre stage.

'The image we have would be impossible for Mickey Mouse to maintain. We're just normal people.'

'We've Only Just Begun', which began life as a bank commercial, consolidated their early success, and the hits kept coming, 'Rainy Days and Mondays', 'Yesterday Once More' and 'Goodbye to Love' helping them achieve 100-million-plus record sales. There was a gruelling touring treadmill, TV specials and even a performance at the White House.

By the mid-1970s the warning signs had begun to appear. Karen reacted to media comments about her weight with a crash-diet regimen, which at times left her too weak to fulfil the duo's exhausting commitments. Anorexia nervosa was not a well-documented condition, and as late as 1981 she was still in denial, responding to questions about her alarming appearance by saying she was 'just pooped'. She also found little joy in a disastrous, short-lived marriage.

On 4 February 1983 Karen Carpenter suffered a fatal heart attack, brought on by her eating disorder. That same year Richard released a new album titled *Voice of the Heart*, deploying unused material from former projects. In 1996 Karen's eponymous solo album, shelved since 1979, finally made it to the record shops.

Top: Richard and Karen, 1974

Right: Karen drums and sings in 1971.

Opposite: On stage at the Royal Festival Hall, London, 1974.

Kurt Cobain

GODFATHER OF GRUNGE
20 FEBRUARY 1967 – 5 APRIL 1994

Kurt Cobain long entertained thoughts that his lot would be the classic rock star arc: fame and acclaim, with a self-inflicted fade-out. He delivered on the first part with the seminal album *Nevermind*; a shotgun took care of the latter.

Kurt Donald Cobain grew up in Aberdeen, Washington, the first-born child of a mechanic father and waitress mother. His parents parted when he was nine, an emotional blow to a hyperactive child who was prescribed Ritalin to control his behaviour. Cobain believed that early pill-popping regimen may have contributed towards the chronic dependency problems that dogged him right up to his death.

Another early development was a morbid fascination with death – a worrying sign in a family with a history of mental health problems and suicide.

As he entered his teens, the guitar and songwriting were Cobain's chief outlets for creative expression. However, profiting from music was still some way off. In the meantime there was a succession of low-grade jobs that barely sustained him.

There were several line-up and name changes before Cobain settled on Nirvana, featuring Krist Novoselic on bass and, from 1990, Dave Grohl on drums. The band

'All my life my dream has been to be a big rock star. Just may as well abuse it while you can.'

released their first single, 'Love Buzz', on the Sub Pop label in November 1988, attracting a cult following both at home and abroad with debut album *Bleach*. They had joined David Geffen's DGC operation by the time *Nevermind* hit the record stores and airwaves in autumn 1991. The set opener 'Smells Like Teen Spirit' – penned by Cobain from a snatch of bedroom graffiti – made the Top 10 on both sides of the Atlantic, while the album, with its dollar-chasing baby on the cover, enjoyed stratospheric sales.

In 1992 Cobain married Courtney Love, who bore him a daughter that year. Fatherhood brought temporary respite from the drug-fuelled dark moods he suffered ('I've always been chronically depressed, or at least pessimistic, for a part of each day'). There were recurring back and stomach problems, too, and Cobain was in poor physical and psychological shape when Nirvana embarked on a world tour to promote their third album, *In Utero*. Munich proved to be the final stop. Cobain returned to his recently purchased mansion near Lake Washington, where he turned a shotgun on himself. In a written note taken to be his parting shot, Cobain chose a Neil Young line: 'It's better to burn out than to fade away.'

Top: Kurt Cobain with Courtney Love and baby Frances Bean in 1993.

Left: Dave Grohl, Kurt Cobain and Krist Novoselic at the 1992 MTV Video Awards.

Opposite: Cobain on stage in 1993.

Ian Curtis

VOICE OF POST-PUNK ALIENATION
15 JULY 1956 – 18 MAY 1980

As lyricist and lead singer of Joy Division, Ian Curtis became the cult band's focal point, delivering his vocals in a trancelike state and dancing like a demented marionette.

Ian Curtis was born in Manchester but spent his formative years in Macclesfield, Cheshire. He set his sights on a music career at an early age, and to that end took a job at a Manchester record store. Rather less rock 'n' roll was his time as a civil servant, which paid the bills while he tried to get a foothold in the business.

In 1976 Curtis was recruited by bass player Peter Hook and guitarist Bernard Sumner, childhood friends who needed a vocalist for the band they were putting together. In May the following year they took to the stage as Warsaw, a nod to their Bowie influences. Stephen Morris replaced the original drummer by the end of the year, when the four-piece outfit reinvented itself as Joy Division, a reference to enforced prostitution at Nazi concentration camps.

Under manager Rob Gretton, the band signed to Tony Wilson's fledgling Factory label. After a limited-release EP came the debut album *Unknown Pleasures* and single 'Transmission'. Both were indie hits, Curtis's raw, uncompromising lyrics resonating with those feeling adrift in a desolate, urban landscape.

> '**Existence – well, what does it matter? I exist on the best terms I can.**'

Below: Ian Curtis with Bernard Sumner on guitar as Joy Division perform in Rotterdam, 1980.

Opposite: Curtis at the Electric Ballroom, London, 1979.

Joy Division attracted a cult following, but even as mainstream success lay within their grasp, Curtis's life was unravelling. He had married his school sweetheart at 19, his wife giving birth to a daughter in 1979. The breakdown of that relationship hit him hard, and his health deteriorated as he began to suffer seizures, sometimes mid-performance. Epilepsy was diagnosed, and the medication needed to keep attacks at bay left its mark in dramatic mood swings. In 'She's Lost Control' he writes movingly about this debilitating condition.

Ian Curtis hanged himself at his Macclesfield home days before the band was due to embark on a US tour. He didn't live to see their best-known song, 'Love Will Tear Us Apart', climb the charts, or the release of their sophomore album *Closer*. The lyrics of the latter scream despair and disintegration and reveal the mindset of a man staring into the abyss – as near a suicide note as anything committed to vinyl, the bleakness of the sentiments both underscored and redeemed by the arresting, effects-laden music.

Bobby Darin

CHAMELEON PERFORMER
14 MAY 1936 – 20 DECEMBER 1973

Bobby Darin was a 1950s teen pop idol who attracted a maturer audience when he remodelled himself as a Sinatra-style nightclub crooner. A composer and multi-instrumentalist, he delivered show tunes and protest songs with equal panache, while his film career brought him Academy recognition.

Born Walden Robert Cassotto and raised in straitened circumstances in the Bronx, Bobby Darin was a man in a hurry. A bout of rheumatic fever in childhood left him with a weakened heart, and he knew his life would be foreshortened. It made him all the more determined to succeed, to pack in as much showbiz success and life experience as possible before his health failed.

With that in mind, Darin quit his theatre studies at New York's Hunter College to pursue a performing career. He formed a writing partnership with Don Kirshner – the brains behind a string of pop successes, including The Monkees – and signed to Decca. But it was after he moved to Atlantic subsidiary Atco that he hit the big time with the 1958 novelty number 'Splish Splash'. It's said he dashed off this million-seller in minutes after being challenged to write a song around that title by DJ Murray the K.

'Queen of the Hop' and 'Dream Lover' were huge follow-up hits, while 'Mack the Knife', taken from Bertolt Brecht and Kurt Weill's *Threepenny Opera*, was the biggest-selling US single of 1959.

By the early 1960s Darin was an established cabaret artist, a regular on the Las Vegas circuit. He also moved into films, sharing the screen with the likes of Sidney Poitier and Steve McQueen, and giving an Oscar-nominated performance in *Captain Newman MD* (1963).

'I want to make it faster than anyone has ever made it before. I'd like to be a legend by the time I'm 25.'

In 1960 he married Sandra Dee, his co-star in *Come September* (1961), a union that lasted seven years.

'Multiplication', 'You Must Have Been a Beautiful Baby' and 'Things' brought further chart success, but that proved elusive after his version of Tim Hardin's 'If I Were a Carpenter' reached the Top 10 in 1966. Albums such as *Commitment* – released in 1969 on his own Direction label – revealed a political dimension that was less commercial, but he returned to the mainstream with a network TV show in the early 1970s.

Bobby Darin was 37 when he died following open-heart surgery in 1973. He was inducted into the Rock and Roll Hall of Fame in 1990, the songwriting equivalent in 1999 and honoured with a Grammy Lifetime Achievement award in 2010.

Below: Bobby Darin and wife Sandra Dee.

Opposite: Darin pictured in the early 1960s.

ACTIVIST AND SINGER-SONGWRITER
31 DECEMBER 1943 – 12 OCTOBER 1997

One of the world's best-loved performers, John Denver earned international acclaim as a singer, lyricist, actor, environmentalist and humanitarian. His music has outlasted countless musical trends and won numerous awards and honours.

Son of an Air Force officer, Henry John Deutschendorf Jr had a disrupted childhood as his family moved from posting to posting. His interest in music came from his maternal grandmother, who gave him his first guitar when he was 11. In 1963 Denver left home, moving to Los Angeles to become involved in the music scene. It was here that he shortened his name, taking his new surname from the capital city of his favourite state, Colorado; later in life, he and his family settled in Aspen and his love for the Rocky Mountains inspired many of his songs.

Denver had his first major break in 1965 when he was chosen as the new lead singer for the popular Mitchell Trio. Two years and three albums later, he had honed his considerable vocal talent and developed his own writing style. He gained wider recognition when his song 'Leaving on a Jet Plane' was recorded by Peter, Paul and Mary, becoming their first and only No 1 hit. By 1969 Denver had left The Mitchell Trio and was climbing up the charts as a solo artist with songs like 'Take Me Home, Country Roads', 'Rocky Mountain High' and 'Annie's Song', becoming one of the top stars of the 1970s.

'Music does bring people together. It allows us to experience the same emotions.'

With the song 'Whose Garden Was This?' Denver was one of the first artists to share an environmental message through his music. He also co-founded the Hunger Project, which is committed to a sustainable end to world hunger, and founded the Windstar Foundation to promote sustainable living. His passion to create a global community led to performances in the USSR and mainland China; he was the first artist from the West to venture into these areas. He returned to the USSR in 1987 to do a benefit concert for the victims of Chernobyl.

In the 1960s, Denver had married Annie Martell – the subject of 'Annie's Song' – and they adopted two children, but by 1982 were divorced. With second wife, Cassandra Delaney, he had a daughter, but this marriage was also over by 1993. Denver was a keen sportsman and loved flying; he died when a plane he was flying crashed into the sea near Pacific Grove, California.

Top: John and Annie Denver photographed in New York, 1980.

Above: Denver photographed in the landscape he loved.

Opposite: John Denver in Southern California, 1990.

23

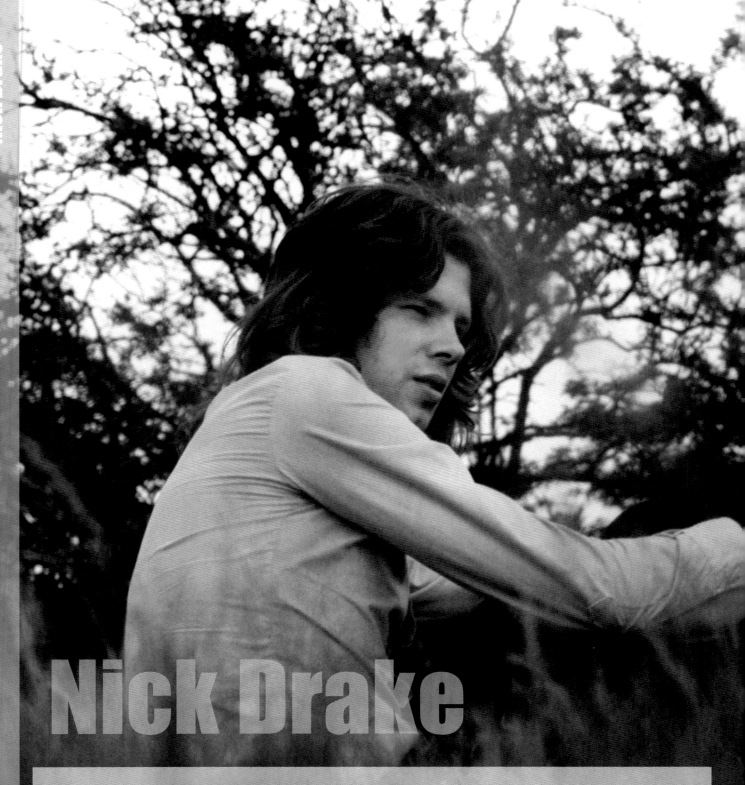

Nick Drake

TORTURED SINGER-SONGWRITER
19 JUNE 1948 – 25 NOVEMBER 1974

In the three albums released during his lifetime, Nick Drake gave the world songs of ethereal beauty. Recognition came too late for this mentally fragile artist, who died from an overdose at 26.

Nick Drake's early years were spent in Burma, where his father worked as an engineer. By the time he reached school age, home was Tanworth-in Arden, a picturesque village in the heart of England. Both Drake's parents were musical, and Nick found his creative outlet in piano and guitar. A high achiever at school, he won a place at Cambridge University to read English, but by then was more interested in developing as a musician than applying himself to his studies.

His break seemed to have come when Fairport Convention's Ashley Hutchings spotted him on the London club circuit. That led to a meeting with producer Joe Boyd, who was equally blown away by Drake's music and helped broker a record deal with Island. The first fruits of that collaboration came with the album *Five Leaves Left*, a work of astonishing maturity for an artist who turned 21 in the year of its release. Fairport Convention's Richard Thompson and Pentangle's Danny Thompson were among the impressive supporting players, but as on all Drake's records, it was the haunting vocals, introspective lyrics and virtuoso guitar-playing that lingered in the memory.

His follow-up long-player, *Bryter Layter*, was a jazzier set, often more playful in tone, yet it was greeted by the same indifference as the debut offering. *Pink Moon*, recorded in just two days, was a pared-down collection, shot through with bleak melancholy. It fared no better.

'I don't want to laugh or cry. I'm numb-dead inside.'

Had Drake had the stagecraft of his actress sister Gabrielle, he might have made a better fist of promoting his work. One reviewer, commenting on a Royal Festival Hall appearance in 1970, marked his talent but noted his lack of stage presence. The shy, sensitive Drake, taciturn at the best of times, couldn't cope with bustling venues, where he was expected to compete with clinking glasses and chatter.

He retreated to his parents' home, a further blow to a man who already perceived himself a failure. Drake became increasingly withdrawn and reliant upon antidepressants, an overdose of which – either accidentally or deliberately administered – ended his life.

Nick Drake's reputation has grown exponentially over the years and he now draws the acclaim that eluded him in life.

Above: Nick Drake is behind the camera in Hampstead, London, in the summer of 1970.

Opposite: A moment of reflection for shy, sensitive Drake, who found it difficult to cope with crowded venues, 1970.

Cass Elliot

MELLIFLUOUS MAMA
19 SEPTEMBER 1941 – 29 JULY 1974

In their brief time together, The Mamas & the Papas served up hits that embraced the mid-1960s freewheeling hippie spirit. Cass Elliot's voice stood out in the soaring four-part harmonies, and she went on to solo success after the group disbanded.

Cass Elliot was the adopted name of Ellen Naomi Cohen, who was born in Baltimore but grew up in Washington, DC. After leaving school, Cass set her sights on an acting career with some success, though in 1962 she lost out to a teenage Barbra Streisand when they were both up for the part of Miss Marmelstein in *I Can Get It For You Wholesale*. From musical theatre she moved into the folk scene, first with The Triumvirate, then The Big 3 after a line-up change. By 1964 she was singing in The Mugwumps, a four-piece whose ranks included Denny Doherty. The 'Mama' billing, which she disliked, was already established, and once The Mamas & the Papas exploded onto the charts, proved impossible to shake off.

Cass was the final piece to be slotted into The Mamas & the Papas jigsaw. In 1965 Husband-and-wife duo John and Michelle Phillips were performing with Doherty, and when Cass went out to the Virgin Islands to join them, the classic line-up was complete. The band's convoluted back story was later told in their transatlantic Top 10 hit 'Creeque Alley'.

Signed to Lou Adler's Dunhill label, The Mamas & the Papas stormed the charts with 'California Dreaming' and 'Monday Monday', the latter hitting top spot in America and bringing them a Grammy. The group's distinctive brand of folk-rock delivered further chart success with 'I Saw Her Again' and a reworking of the Shirelles' 'Dedicated to the One I Love'. The four were somewhat less harmonious when they weren't performing, and by 1968 Cass was keen to break free from the shackles of band membership. Her version of 'Dream a Little Dream of Me' gave the group their final hit and launched her solo career.

'When I heard us sing together the first time, we knew – this is it.'

Songs such as 'It's Getting Better' and 'Make Your Own Kind of Music', cabaret and TV appearances – including her own prime-time specials – showed that Cass had the star quality to make it on her own. None of the other band members enjoyed such success, short-lived though it was. She had just finished a two-week engagement playing to packed houses at the London Palladium when she died from a heart attack, aged 32.

Below: The Mamas & the Papas: (L–R) Denny Doherty, Mama Cass Elliot, Michelle Phillips and John Phillips.

Opposite: Cass parades for the camera in a promotional shoot for her television special Don't Call Me Mama Anymore *in September 1973.*

Marvin Gaye

PRINCE OF MOTOWN
2 APRIL 1939 – 1 APRIL 1984

Marvin Gaye's blend of R & B and pop came to epitomize the 'Motown sound'. Later he moved to an intensely personal form of social commentary, which redefined soul music's creative force and its influence for social change, and finally to sensual songs that celebrated sexual appeal.

Born in Washington, DC, Marvin Pentz Gay Jr – he added the 'e' later – was the son of a minister in a strict religious order. Young Gaye was expected to follow his domineering father into the church, but was encouraged by his mother to develop his musical talents. To escape his father he joined the US Air Force, but his growing dislike of authority caused an early discharge. Blessed with a wide vocal range that spanned three styles – a piercing falsetto, a smooth

mid-range tenor and a deep gospel growl – Gaye was part of several groups before being signed by Motown. His first major hit, 'Pride & Joy', came in 1963, following which he enjoyed growing success – but came to dislike the material he was performing.

In 1967 Gaye was partnered musically with Tammi Terrell, which was a great success; but she collapsed in

Left: Motown star Diana Ross poses with Marvin Gaye in 1973.

Above: Marvin Gaye poses on a scooter, circa 1967.

Opposite: Gaye holds his award for 'Sexual Healing' at the 1983 Grammys.

'**If you cannot find peace within yourself, you will never find it anywhere else.**'

his arms on stage towards the end of the year and was diagnosed with a brain tumour. He was deeply upset, attempting suicide at one point and refusing to do live gigs after her death in 1970. That year he collaborated on 'What's Going On', but Motown at first refused to release it, fearing its political and anti-Vietnam War stance would cause a backlash. When it finally came out it quickly topped the charts; Gaye produced a follow-up album, *What's Going On*, a collection of jazz-influenced songs inspired by life in America's black urban neighbourhoods that became the most significant work of his career. He overdubbed his voice three or four times to provide a rich harmony, a technique he employed for the rest of his career.

Later Gaye abandoned social commentary for sensuality, releasing *Let's Get It On* in 1973, after which he was reluctantly pushed into a tour. By the end of the 1970s, with a growing addiction to cocaine and deeply in debt for back taxes, he fled the United States for exile in Europe. Here he wrote 'Sexual Healing', a song that sat at No 1 for ten weeks and led to two Grammy awards. Back in Los Angeles Gaye moved into his parents' home for a break from the music business, but during a family conflict Marvin Sr shot and killed his son.

Andy Gibb

THE FOURTH BEE GEE
5 MARCH 1958 – 10 MARCH 1988

In the late 1970s Andy Gibb eclipsed the success of his three elder brothers, becoming the first solo male artist to top the *Billboard* Hot 100 with his first three singles.

In the year of his birth, Andy Gibb's family swapped the northwest of England for Australia, where elder brothers Barry, Robin and Maurice made their mark in the pop world. By the time he celebrated his tenth birthday, the Bee Gees were UK chart-toppers, and Andy soon began to show that he, too, had inherited his parents' musicality. He picked up the guitar and had a voice with the distinctive Gibb timbre. Teen-idol looks were no hindrance.

He cut his performing teeth in clubs on Ibiza and the Isle of Man, both family bases during the early 1970s. Back in his homeland Gibb scored his first hit with 'Words and Music', released on the ATA label. 1976 brought a marriage that lasted just two years, but professionally it proved to be a turning point as he signed with Robert Stigwood, the entertainment entrepreneur who had guided the Bee Gees to the top. 'I Just Want To Be Your Everything', Gibb's debut single for Stigwood's RSO label, stormed the US charts. It made the lower reaches of the UK Top 40, an early indication that America was to be the main locus of his popularity.

1978 was his golden year in terms of chart success. '(Love is) Thicker Than Water' – co-written with Barry – hit the top spot, supplanting the Bee Gees' 'Stayin' Alive'. 'Shadow Dancing', the title track from his biggest-selling album, followed suit, while 'An Everlasting Love' made the Top 10 on both sides of the Atlantic. '(Our Love) Don't Throw It All Away', another million-seller, meant Gibb had four of America's Top 100 singles of 1978.

> **'There is nothing to compare with the instantaneous feedback a singer gets from the people sitting in front of him.'**

Left: Andy Gibb with girlfriend and actress Victoria Principal, circa 1982.

Above: With brothers Barry, Robin and Maurice at the Billboard Music Awards in 1977.

Opposite: Andy Gibb was the youngest boy of five children; the famous brothers had one sister, Lesley.

He duetted with Olivia Newton-John on 'I Can't Help It', and with then-girlfriend Victoria Principal in a rendition of 'All I Have to do is Dream'. He also showed his versatility by taking to the stage in *Pirates of Penzance* and *Joseph and the Amazing Technicolor Dreamcoat*. Hosting the TV show *Solid Gold* seemed to provide further proof that he would take the end of disco in his stride. But a cocaine habit rendered him a liability, and he lost both his television job and the Broadway lead in *Joseph* after going awol once too often. The hits also dried up, and in 1987 he filed for bankruptcy. Gibb was attempting to re-ignite his music career in Britain when he died from myocarditis, five days after celebrating his 30th birthday.

Jimi Hendrix

PEERLESS GUITARIST
27 NOVEMBER 1942 – 18 SEPTEMBER 1970

Jimi Hendrix was an undiscovered talent in his native America, backing a host of big-name acts before crossing the Atlantic and becoming one of the biggest of them all.

He was born Johnny Allen Hendrix, renamed James Marshall by his father, called himself Jimmy James as an unknown on the club circuit and finally adopted the Jimi moniker when he was on the cusp of fame. The changes are apposite for someone whose life can be broken down into several distinct phases. Jimi was the rock god whose guitar playing blew away the likes of Jeff Beck and Eric Clapton. A quarter of a century earlier, Johnny Allen Hendrix grew up in Seattle, where his father worked as a gardener. The left-handed youngster taught himself to play, acquiring a right-handed guitar and flipping it upside down. A natural feel for the instrument and a finely tuned ear aided his development. 'You've got to know much more than just the technicalities of

Below: The Jimi Hendrix Experience, (L–R) Noel Redding, Jimi Hendrix and Mitch Mitchell, pose for a group portrait in March 1967 in Hamburg, Germany.

Opposite: Hendrix performing on stage playing his white Fender Stratocaster guitar.

notes,' he once said. 'You've got to know what goes between the notes.' He never learned to read or write music.

Influenced by blues legends, such as Robert Johnson and Howlin' Wolf, Hendrix quit school early and joined several R & B bands before enlisting in 1961. The next year saw Hendrix in paratrooper mode, a member of the 101st Airborne Division. After being invalided out in 1962, he joined the session and support circuit, a jobbing instrumentalist for artists including Little Richard, the Isley Brothers and Curtis Mayfield. By 1966 he was based in New York, and it was while performing in a Greenwich Village club in July that Hendrix's fortunes took a significant turn. Now a front man performing as Jimmy James, with his Blue Flames backing band, Hendrix came to the attention of The Animals' bass player Chas Chandler. He knew he had witnessed something special, and two months later brought Hendrix to England with a view to giving him the platform his talent warranted.

Noel Redding was recruited to play bass, Mitch Mitchell on drums, and the three-piece Jimi Hendrix Experience took their stage bow in France in October 1966. Even before the release of their debut single, 'Hey Joe', the music scene cognoscenti knew about Hendrix. There was the singing voice, which he thought

indifferent, though fans begged to differ; there was the look: frizzy-haired, mustachioed and every inch the flower-power-era rock star. But most of all there was the guitar playing. He combined rhythm and lead, plucked the strings with his teeth, whirled his Fender Stratocaster behind his back and took to setting it alight. In others it might have been mere stage gimmickry; with Hendrix it was the real deal. The sounds he was able to produce, using feedback, distortion and effects, such as the recently developed wah-wah pedal, put him in a class of his own.

The follow-up singles 'Purple Haze', 'The Wind Cries Mary' and Dylan's 'All Along The Watchtower' all made the UK Top 10. The last of those gave him his only Top 20 hit in his homeland. The debut album *Are You Experienced* was released in May 1967, peaking at No 2 in the United Kingdom and remaining on the chart

> '*I feel guilty when people say I'm the greatest on the scene. What's good or bad doesn't matter to me; what does matter is feeling and not feeling.*'

for 33 weeks. The Beatles' *Sergeant Pepper* deprived the group of top spot.

Hendrix returned to the United States a star, making a huge splash at the Monterey Pop Festival in June 1967. His set included a brilliant version of 'Wild Thing', and there were the usual pyrotechnics. The Experience backed The Monkees on tour that summer, one of the less likely concert pairings. In January the following year Hendrix embarked on a major US tour on the back of the release of his second album, *Axis: Bold as Love*, which made the Top 10 on both sides of the Atlantic. He was beginning to tire of the showy displays expected of him, and internal cracks began to manifest themselves.

The group's final album, the double set *Electric Ladyland*, featured a number of guest contributors, including Steve Winwood. The Experience played their last gig in June 1969, though Mitchell was still on board in a new line-up that closed Woodstock two months later. This was the show where he gave his famous rendition of 'The Star-Spangled Banner'.

Hendrix formed the all-black Band of Gypsys, which survived just long enough to put out an eponymous album, then started work on a new project, *First Rays of the New Rising Sun*, unreleased until 1997. He died two weeks after playing the Isle of Wight Festival, at girlfriend Monika Danneman's London flat. Inhalation of vomit was the cause of death.

'Voodoo Chile' gave Jimi Hendrix a posthumous No 1, the position he holds in the pantheon of rock guitarists in the view of many fans and fellow axemen.

Opposite left: Hendrix and Mitchell in a recording studio in October 1968.

Opposite top: Hendrix performs during the Woodstock Festival, August 1969.

Right: With Hendrix confirmed in the line-up for the 1970 Isle of Wight Festival, artists such as Chicago, The Doors, The Who, Joan Baez and Free took up the chance to play there.

Buddy Holly

PIONEER OF ROCK AND POP
7 SEPTEMBER 1936 – 3 FEBRUARY 1959

Buddy Holly was a major recording star for just two years, yet he influenced a generation of artists. Paul McCartney bought Holly's catalogue and backed an annual festival celebrating the life and work of one of his musical heroes. The Stones' first Top 10 hit was a cover of Holly's 'Not Fade Away'. And on 'American Pie' Don McLean described Holly's untimely death as 'the day the music died'.

Charles Hardin Holley was born and raised in Lubbock, Texas. The nickname 'Buddy' was soon settled upon within the family unit, while the 'e' in his surname was dropped accidentally much later, the result of a transcription error on a recording contract. Holly's mother and older siblings were all musical, and Buddy dabbled with violin and piano, as well as steel-string guitar and banjo. When he got together with school pal Bob Montgomery – performing as Buddy and Bob – country and bluegrass dominated the set list. The duo became well known on the local circuit, gigging regularly and even getting a radio spot. That all changed after Elvis burst onto the scene. Holly had seen the future: rock 'n' roll and the electric guitar.

A talent scout saw enough to get him an audition at Decca in late 1955. Over the next year Holly made a number of recordings in Nashville and cut a couple of country-style singles that barely raised a ripple. Decca decided to pass when the option of a contract renewal fell due. Holly responded by heading to the indie studio run by Norman Petty in Clovis, New Mexico. There, in February 1957, he recorded the self-penned 'That'll Be the Day', the title taken from John Wayne's common refrain in his recently released western *The Searchers*.

With Petty installed as manager, success lay just around the corner, and it coincided with a settling of both the line-up and the band name. The group had gone through several incarnations, with a revolving door

Opposite: Charles Hardin Holley, New York City, 1958.

Below: Buddy Holly and The Crickets, (L–R) Joe B. Mauldin, Buddy Holly, Jerry Allison and Niki Sullivan, pose for a group shot on the set of the BBC television show Off The Record *during their UK tour, 1958.*

of backing players. Now, after a rogue chirruping noise found its way onto a recording, it was decided that Buddy would be supported by The Crickets: drummer Jerry Allison, guitarist Niki Sullivan and newly recruited bass player Joe B. Mauldin. Sullivan soon departed, leaving the classic three-piece line-up of the brief, golden era.

'That'll Be the Day' didn't take off immediately. A few labels turned it down before Coral – ironically, a Decca subsidiary – showed an interest. It was eventually released on Brunswick, another Decca offshoot. The single topped the charts on both sides of the Atlantic, and in September 1957 the follow-up 45 'Peggy Sue' hit the airwaves. Originally titled 'Cindy Lou', it had been renamed to give Allison's girlfriend Peggy Sue Gerron her own piece of pop immortality. Internal politics meant that the song was issued under Holly's

Left and below: Buddy Holly and The Crickets appear on Ed Sullivan's CBS variety show Toast of the Town, *New York, December 1957.*

'We like this kind of music. Jazz is strictly for stay-at-homes.'

Backed by a new group, including the unknown Waylon Jennings on bass, Holly set out on a three-week tour of the Midwest in January 1959. Also on the bill were teen sensation Ritchie Valens, who had recently scored a huge hit with 'Donna' and 'La Bamba', and the Big Bopper, best known for 'Chantilly Lace'. After performing in Clear Lake, Iowa, they and Holly took off from Mason City Airport in a chartered single-engine Beechcraft Bonanza. They were bound for North Dakota and the next gig, happy for a brief respite from an unreliable, unheated tour bus. The plane crashed shortly after take-off; there were no survivors.

Holly had a posthumous No 1 with the Paul Anka-penned 'It Doesn't Matter Anymore', while the first of numerous compilation LPs, *The Buddy Holly Story*, was soon in the charts, where it remained for three years.

Above: Following a performance when opening for Bill Haley & His Comets, Decca Records signed Holley to a contract in February 1956, misspelling his name as Holly.

Right: Holly poses with Red Robinson, the first Canadian disc jockey to play rock 'n' roll.

name alone on Coral, to whom he was contracted. Others went out on the Brunswick label, which had The Crickets' signatures. The fans didn't care. It was a fresh, vibrant sound, the bespectacled front man didn't look like a typical pop star and his voice – complete with trademark hiccup – was equally distinctive.

In December 1957 the group performed both hits on the prestigious *Ed Sullivan Show*. The new year saw The Crickets tour Australia and the United Kingdom, where they went down a storm. It was a breathless schedule of performing and studio work, and the hits kept coming. 'Oh Boy', 'Maybe Baby' and 'Rave On' all made the Top 40 in the United States, the Top 10 in the United Kingdom. Holly also found time to fall in love and get married, to Maria Elena Santiago. His bride lived in New York, and in the autumn of 1958 Holly decided to make the Big Apple his home, splitting from The Crickets and Petty. 'Heartbeat' was the first release without his usual accompanists, who returned to Texas and continued performing without the star turn.

Michael Hutchence

AUSSIE ROCK GOD
22 JANUARY 1960 – 22 NOVEMBER 1997

Michael Hutchence fronted Australia's most successful rock band. His vocal performance was underpinned by an animal magnetism and raw sexuality that lit up INXS's stage shows as they stormed the charts in the 1980s.

Michael Hutchence was born in Sydney but spent most of his childhood years in Hong Kong, where his father had business interests. Back in Sydney by the age of 12, he befriended Andrew Farriss, with whom he would form a productive writing partnership. Farriss was the superior instrumentalist, while Hutchence revealed a flair for language in his poetic offerings. There was a hiatus in their relationship when Michael's parents divorced and he went to live with his make-up artist mother in California. Music became his central concern after he returned and reconnected with Farriss. Bass

'Fame makes me feel wanted and loved – anybody wants that.'

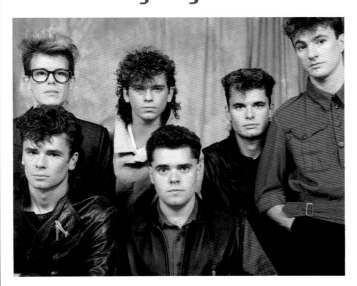

player Garry Beers came on board, and later Farriss's brothers Tim and Jon joined the band, along with guitarist-saxophonist Kirk Pengilly.

They took to the circuit as The Farriss Brothers ('We played every bar, party, pub, hotel lounge, church hall, mining town – places that made Mad Max territory look like a Japanese garden'). In 1980 the band, rebadged INXS, landed a recording deal and scored well with singles such as 'Just Keep Walking' and albums *Underneath the Colours* and *Shabooh Shoobah*. The latter set included 'The One Thing', which played well in the United States, though their first big Stateside hit came in 1986 with 'What You Need'. The 1987 album *Kick* was a monster success, spawning the worldwide hit single 'Need You Tonight'.

Hutchence branched out into film acting with *Dogs in Space* and *Frankenstein Unbound*, but in the 1990s, as the group's popularity seemed to be waning, his private life took centre stage. Celebrity partners included supermodel Helena Christensen and pop diva Kylie Minogue. His relationship with British TV personality Paula Yates sparked an acrimonious divorce and custody battle between Yates and husband Bob Geldof, which intensified after she gave birth to Hutchence's daughter in 1996. Even with a new album

Left: INXS studio group portrait: L–R (back) Kirk Pengilly, Michael Hutchence, Jon Farriss, Garry Beers, (front) Tim Farriss, Andrew Farriss, circa 1983.

Opposite: On stage in San José, California, 1994.

and talks with Tarantino in the melting pot, it was said that he was deeply depressed by the protracted wrangling and tabloid onslaught it provoked. Matters were unresolved when Hutchence was found hanged in a Sydney hotel room, the coroner recording a verdict of suicide while under the influence of drugs and alcohol. The circumstances surrounding his death led some experts – and Yates – to conclude that he may have been a victim of autoerotic asphyxiation.

Michael Jackson

KING OF POP
29 AUGUST 1958 – 25 JUNE 2009

Michael Jackson embarked on the road to superstardom when most children were starting school. He fronted The Jackson 5 and carved out a phenomenally successful solo career, but his personal life was less charmed. His eccentricities came under the spotlight, though his legions of fans prefer to remember the music and dazzling performances of one of pop's great showmen.

Michael was the seventh of nine children born to Joe and Katherine Jackson. Home was Gary, Indiana, and it was on the local talent circuit that five of the brothers began to make a name for themselves in the mid-1960s. Jackie, Tito, Jermaine and Marlon were the other members of the group that eventually branded themselves The Jackson 5, but it soon became clear that

Below: The Jackson 5 strut their stuff on the Bob Hope Special in 1973. Michael was already struggling to cope with the adulation that came with being the star turn of the group.

Opposite: Jackson appears relaxed in front of the cameras in London in 1983.

there was just one candidate for lead singer. Joe's hand was firmly on the tiller. He had once harboured musical ambitions of his own, and was a stern taskmaster. The boys made their first recordings on minor local label Steeltown, signing to Motown in 1968. With the backing of Berry Gordy's slick machine, including some top in-house writers, The Jackson 5 were on their way. 'I Want You Back', released in October 1969, went to the top of the *Billboard* chart, followed by 'ABC', 'The Love You Save' and 'I'll Be There'. 'I'll Be There' was the top-selling single of 1970 in the United States and the group's biggest hit, while 11-year-old Michael became the youngest singer to have a No 1 record.

three monster album successes. *Off the Wall* included 'Don't Stop 'Til You Get Enough', 'She's Out of My Life' and the Rod Temperton-penned 'Rock With You'. The ex-Heatwave member would write some of Jackson's biggest hits, including the title track of his next album, *Thriller*. It topped the US chart for 37 weeks, yielded seven Top 10 hits and walked off with seven Grammys en route to becoming the biggest-selling album of all time. The John Landis-directed video also broke new ground for the fledgling MTV generation.

Above: Wearing the trademark one glove, Michael performs on the 1984 Victory tour.

Right: Pictured on the second leg of the 1988 Bad tour, which grossed a record $125 million.

Modelling himself on James Brown, Jackson gained widespread admiration for his soulful rendition of lyrics that should have been beyond the compass of youth. His solo career launched in 1971 with 'Got To Be There', and he scored his first chart-topper the following year with 'Ben', an unlikely ballad whose subject was a pet rat.

Desiring more creative control, the brothers signed to Epic in 1976, rebadging themselves The Jacksons as Motown had legal ownership of their former name. Songs such as 'Enjoy Yourself' sold well, and 'Show You the Way to Go' gave them their only UK No 1. It wasn't until their third Epic album, *Destiny*, that they got the chance to self-produce. That album spawned classic disco-era hits 'Shake Your Body Down to the Ground' and 'Blame it on the Boogie'. Increasingly, Michael's solo work took precedence, and appearing with his brothers was a concession that boosted their flagging careers just as his went into overdrive.

On the set of *The Wiz*, an all-black production of *The Wizard of Oz* in which Michael played the Scarecrow, Jackson befriended the film's musical director Quincy Jones. Over the next decade the two collaborated on

change of appearance, which he put down to a rare skin condition. A short-lived marriage to Lisa Marie Presley followed lurid improper conduct charges involving a teenager. The case was dropped but money changed hands, which didn't look good. He was cleared of similar allegations a decade later, by which time Jackson was father to three children. Two were the product of another brief marriage, while the identity of the woman who bore Prince Michael Jackson II was not revealed.

The four-month court case took a heavy toll, and Jackson was not in the rudest of health. An addiction to painkillers may have dated back to the second-degree burns he suffered while making a Pepsi-Cola commercial in 1984. Some insiders thought he was not up to doing the comeback shows planned for summer 2009, a view tragically endorsed when on 25 June he collapsed at his California home. When he appeared in London in March to announce the O2 Arena concerts Jackson had said, 'This is it … the final curtain call', words that took on a grim reality three months later.

'My goal in life is to give to the world what I was lucky to receive: the ecstasy of divine union through my music and my dance.'

Jackson unveiled his moonwalk in 1983, and his single-gloved, crotch-grabbing routines made his concerts as memorable visually as they were musically. *Bad* was always going to suffer in comparison to *Thriller*, but still delivered a record five US No 1s following its release in 1987. Jackson also co-authored 'We Are the World', a worldwide hit that raised millions for famine relief.

In the 1990s the successes were fewer and further between and it was Jackson's lifestyle that became more newsworthy. There was an unusual line in pets, a home complete with amusement park and a startling

Top left: Jackson with Lisa Marie Presley. The pair married in May 1994 but the marriage was short-lived, ending in August 1996.

Above: Jackson performs a routine from the show celebrating his 30 years as a solo artist in 2001.

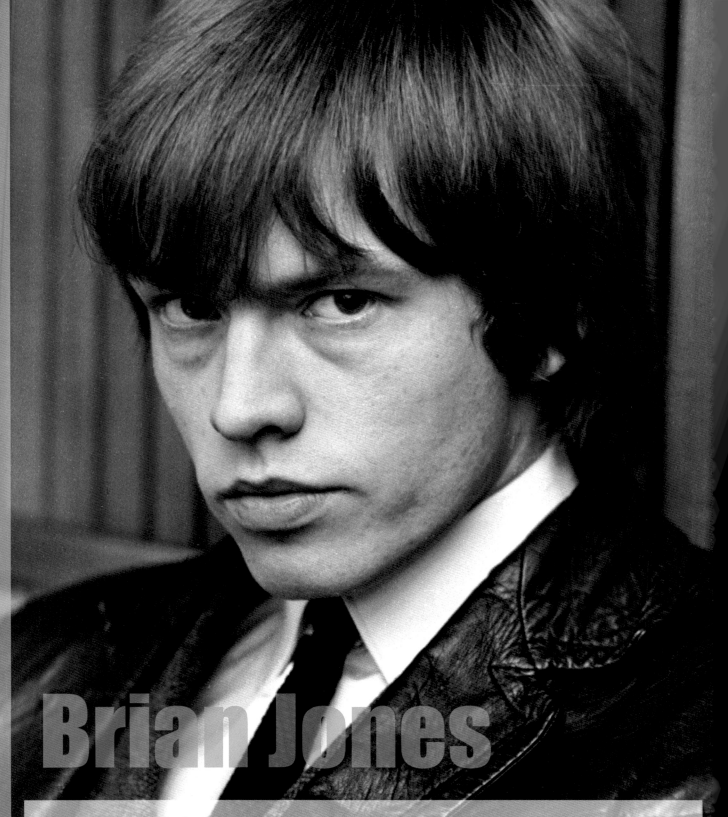

Brian Jones

ROLLING STONES' FOUNDING FATHER
28 FEBRUARY 1942 – 3 JULY 1969

A gifted multi-instrumentalist and de facto leader of the Rolling Stones during their early days, Brian Jones became increasingly marginalized as the decade wore on and died shortly after leaving the group in 1969.

Brian Jones had a middle-class upbringing in Cheltenham, Gloucestershire. He did well academically, and took his first musical steps on piano and clarinet. A rebellious streak appeared in his teenage years, and after taking A-levels, Jones chose employment over university. The role of office junior in the architect's department of the local council didn't stimulate a restless young man looking for direction and inspiration. He found both after a chance meeting with Alexis Korner, who invited Jones to look him up if he came to London. In 1961 Korner had formed Blues Incorporated, featuring Charlie Watts on drums, and a year later opened the Ealing R & B Club, which became a magnet for blues fans. Jones was soon in that circle, as were Mick Jagger and Keith Richards.

In the early days Jones billed himself as Elmo Lewis, a nod to slide guitar legend Elmore James. He came to Jagger and Richards's attention after guesting for Korner's band, and in spring 1962 the three formed the Rollin' Stones, taking their name from a Muddy Waters song. There were a few personnel changes before Watts and bassist Bill Wyman came on board to complete the classic five-piece line-up, which signed to Decca and debuted with a cover of Chuck Berry's 'Come On' in June 1963.

The flamboyant Jones played an array of instruments in a group that scored seven UK chart-toppers. 'Not Fade Away' gave them their first Stateside Top 10 hit, while '(I Can't Get No) Satisfaction' was the biggest-selling US single of 1965.

Andrew Loog Oldham's arrival as manager undermined Jones's role, as did the emergence of the Jagger-Richards songwriting partnership. Jones became increasingly dependent on drugs and alcohol. The sensitive, mentally fragile Jones also had to cope when girlfriend Anita Pallenberg left him for Richards.

A month after leaving the group in June 1969, Brian Jones drowned during a midnight swim in the pool of his Sussex home. The Stones, complete with new recruit Mick Taylor, played Hyde Park 48 hours later, which became a memorial concert. Jagger read Shelley's poem *Adonais*, and 3,000 white butterflies were released. *Rolling Stone* magazine provided its own epitaph: 'If Keith and Mick were the mind and body of the Stones, Brian was clearly the soul'.

'We've come along with a very raw sort of music, where everything was rather sweet.'

Below left: The Rolling Stones in 1964: (L–R) Bill Wyman, Charlie Watts, Keith Richards, Mick Jagger and Brian Jones.

Below: Jones with Anita Pallenberg in 1966.

Opposite: Jones is reluctant to smile for the camera in 1963.

Janis Joplin

ROCK GODDESS
19 JANUARY 1943 – 4 OCTOBER 1970

Janis Joplin was a white girl who sang the blues in singular style, a rock wild child whose excesses matched any of her male counterparts. She crashed and burned barely three years after her star-making performance at the Monterey International Pop Festival.

Janis Joplin had little affection for her home town of Port Arthur, Texas. She was a misfit at school, the butt of boys' jibes, who found solace in art and books, and then the blues. Having experienced loneliness and desolation, she readily connected with the music of Leadbelly, Bessie Smith and their ilk. Joplin started singing in bars during her time at the University of

Texas and headed for California in 1963, happy to put her first 20 years behind her. She would pour out a lot of the hurt of those early years in the song 'Little Girl Blue'.

> 'I can't talk about my singing; I'm inside it. How can you describe something you're inside of?'

Joplin felt at home in the beatnik-bohemian scene of San Francisco's Haight-Ashbury, epicentre of hippie counterculture. There she eked out a living, singing on the local circuit for beers or passing round the hat. By 1966 she was performing in Big Brother and the Holding Company, whose breakthrough came at Monterey the following summer. Joplin's performance, including a rendition of Big Mama Thornton's 'Ball and Chain', wowed the crowd, and she was soon attracting media attention as the star of the group. Big Brother struck a deal with Dylan's manager Albert Grossman and signed to Columbia, a huge fanfare accompanying the release of their album *Cheap Thrills* in August 1968. It had advance sales enough to guarantee gold certification and included another Joplin standard, 'Piece of My Heart'.

By the end of the year, internal tensions spilled over and Joplin left to form The Kozmic Blues Band. That outfit remained together just long enough to put out the album *I Got Dem Ol' Kozmic Blues Again*

Above and opposite: Singer, songwriter, painter, dancer and music arranger, Janis Joplin rose to prominence in the late 1960s as the lead singer of Big Brother and the Holding Company.

Mama!. Joplin again moved on, fronting The Full Tilt Boogie Band in 1970, with whom she recorded her best known long-player, *Pearl*. It featured Kris Kristofferson's 'Me and Bobby McGee', which gave her a posthumous hit on the singles chart, and her unaccompanied 'Mercedes-Benz', which became a signature work.

Joplin's private life was spinning out of control. At Woodstock in 1969 her spot was delayed to give her time to recover from a drink-and-drugs cocktail. She still looked out of it on stage. Work on *Pearl* was all but complete when she succumbed to her final fix, accidental heroin overdose the official ruling on her death, aged 27.

49

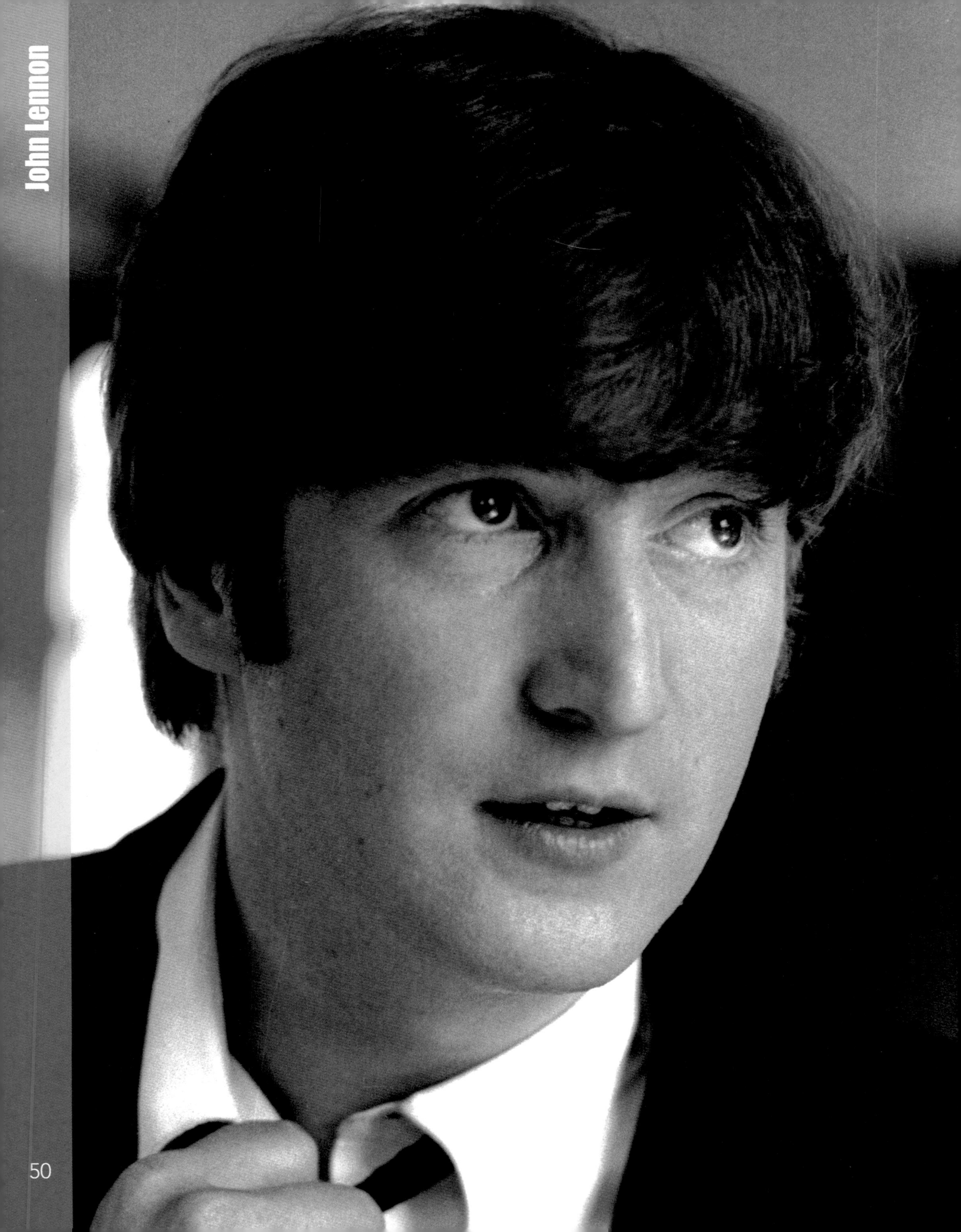

John Lennon

WORKING CLASS HERO
9 OCTOBER 1940 – 8 DECEMBER 1980

As one half of the creative genius behind The Beatles, John Lennon was a towering figure on the cultural map, revered for a cornucopia of artistic triumphs and as standard-bearer for the peace-and-love generation.

John Winston Lennon was born in turbulent times, his home city of Liverpool enduring nightly bombing raids as the Luftwaffe sought to inflict damage on one of the country's key ports. His father, Freddie, was a merchant seaman, absent for long periods but not the feckless family deserter he would often be painted as in the Lennon story. He and John's mother, Julia, drifted apart, a breach hastened by the fact that she became pregnant by another man during one of Freddie's trips. John's half-sister, born in June 1945, was given up for adoption.

Julia took up with a new lover, who was unenthusiastic about raising another man's child. Thus, John was ushered into the welcoming arms of his mother's sister – his beloved Aunt Mimi – and from the age of five enjoyed a stable, contented childhood in a leafy Liverpool suburb. In his teens John was in regular contact with Julia, who encouraged his interest in music and taught him some banjo chords. When he caught the skiffle bug, she bought him a guitar. Julia died in July 1958, hit by a car on her way home from visiting Mimi. At 17 John had lost his mother for a second time.

At Quarry Bank School John showed his rebellious streak, preferring comic doodlings, surreal flights of fancy and nonsense verse to jumping through academic hoops. His undoubted talent needed an outlet, which arrived in the form of rock 'n' roll. 'Nothing really affected me until Elvis,' he said. Like countless other

Right: John, Paul, George and Ringo take part in The Morecambe and Wise Show *in December 1963.*

Opposite: John pictured in 1964. By any standards 1963 had been a remarkable year for The Beatles but at the beginning of 1964 they were ready to launch themselves on the world stage.

51

teenagers, John formed a band, and at a village fete gig on 6 July 1957 the historic meeting with Paul McCartney took place. The latter was a threat to Lennon's position as group leader but his talent could move The Quarrymen forward. The two were soon striking creative sparks off each other, honing the songwriting skills that would make their catalogue the most valuable commodity in the business. Shortly after Ringo completed the line-up and 'Love Me Do' gave The Beatles their first chart success in autumn 1962, John and Paul settled on a Lennon-McCartney credit for all their output, whether it was a collaborative or solo effort.

John and Paul proved themselves masters of the three-minute pop song with a hooky tune and lyrics working the boy-girl theme from every angle. 'Please Please Me', 'She Loves You' and 'I Want to Hold Your Hand' were among the monster hits that stormed the charts and sent fans into raptures. But having reached 'the toppermost of the poppermost', as John described their quest for fame and fortune, he soon tired of the formulaic songs and adulation. Neither marriage to Cynthia nor fatherhood brought fulfilment. Lennon's songs became introspective and confessional – 'Help!' was a naked plea as well as a catchy title song for a movie. His remark that The Beatles were 'more popular than Jesus' prompted a Bible Belt backlash that made their final tour of the USA in summer 1966 an unsettling experience. Freddie emerged from the shadows, but the childhood ghosts were difficult to lay to rest. John

'If everyone demanded peace instead of another television set, then there'd be peace.'

when John's anthemic 'Give Peace a Chance' charted under the Plastic Ono Band banner, signalling the way forward before The Beatles' dissolution was confirmed. John and Yoko made headlines with their bed-ins and 'bagism', while his seminal *Imagine* album showed that new recordings weren't to be monopolized by avant-garde sound collages.

In 1971 John and Yoko decamped to New York, which seemed to offer greater freedom. Lennon returned to the golden age of rock 'n' roll for inspiration, but music took a back seat for five years following the birth of son Sean in 1975. He became the hands-on father that Beatlemania had made impossible with first-born son Julian. Lennon returned with *Double Fantasy* in 1980, released a month before he was struck down by gunshots outside the Dakota, his apartment building. His assassin, 25-year-old Mark Chapman, had a history of mental illness. He made no attempt to evade justice, pleaded guilty and was given 20 years to life.

Opposite: The Beatles took New York by storm in 1964.

Above: In 1966 Lennon played the part of Private Gripweed in Dick Lester's black comedy How I Won the War.

Right: John and Yoko attend John's first art exhibition, 1968.

would later undertake Primal Scream therapy to address deep-seated issues of abandonment.

Songs such as 'Strawberry Fields Forever', 'I Am the Walrus' and 'Lucy in the Sky with Diamonds' show Lennon's development as a writer. If McCartney was the master of melody, he was the wordsmith, his inventive imagery and caustic wit coursing through two published volumes – *In His Own Write* (1964) and *A Spaniard in the Works (1965)* – as well as his lyrics.

There was drug and alcohol abuse, and a flirtation with transcendental meditation as John sought to imbue his life with greater meaning. It arrived in the shape of Japanese conceptual artist Yoko Ono, whom he described as 'me in drag'. They married in 1969,

Bob Marley

REGGAE SUPERSTAR
6 FEBRUARY 1945 – 11 MAY 1981

As front man of the Wailers, Bob Marley chalked up numerous hits in Jamaica before achieving worldwide fame in the 1970s. No other Third World artist had made such a global impact on the music scene.

Nesta Robert Marley was born in Jamaica's Saint Ann parish, the son of British army captain Norval Marley and native Jamaican Cedella Malcolm. The marriage soon foundered. Norval had little contact with Bob, while Cedella later remarried and moved to Wilmington, Delaware. Before emigrating she had a daughter by Taddeus Livingston, whose son, nicknamed Bunny, shared Bob's musical ambitions.

In 1963 they founded the original Wailers, along with Peter Tosh, Junior Braithwaite, Beverley Kelso and Cherry Smith. Marley had already cut a couple of discs that raised barely a ripple. Now, recording for Clement 'Sir Coxsone' Dodd's Studio One label, things took off as songs such as 'Simmer Down' and 'It Hurts to Be Alone' put them on the local map.

'Don't just move to the music, listen to what I'm saying.'

At the height of his fame Marley was struck down by cancer. Shortly before his death he was awarded Jamaica's Order of Merit, having already received the UN Peace Medal of the Third World.

Marley's life and work were informed by his commitment to Rastafarianism, his songs voicing the concerns of the deprived and downtrodden. He lives on through his music, notably through the 1984 compilation album *Legend*, a multiple-platinum seller and by some distance the most commercially successful reggae album in history.

Left: Bob and the original Wailers photographed in Jamaica in 1972: (L–R) Bunny Wailer, Bob Marley, Carlton Barrett, Peter Tosh and Aston 'Family Man' Barrett.

Below: Marley in Los Angeles during the Survival tour, 1979.

Opposite: Marley at Crystal Palace, London, in 1980.

By 1966, Kelso, Smith and Braithwaite had all departed, while Marley married Rita Anderson, a future Wailers' backing singer. Achieving chart success in Jamaica brought little material gain. Marley took a number of manual jobs, including a spell on the Chrysler assembly line while visiting his mother.

There was a fertile collaborative period with producer Lee 'Scratch' Perry and the Barrett brothers, Aston and Carlton, the latter duo enhancing The Wailers' rhythm section. But the breakthrough came when the group signed to Island Records in 1972. Their debut album, *Catch a Fire*, sold well enough, while the follow-up, *Burnin'*, was boosted by Clapton's cover of 'I Shot the Sheriff'. The next long-player, *Natty Dread*, spawned the hit single 'No Woman No Cry'. The group's fan base was wide, Marley establishing himself as a major crossover artist. *Exodus*, *Kaya* and *Survival* had huge worldwide sales, while 'Jamming', 'One Love' and 'Could You Be Loved' added to the tally of hit singles.

Freddie Mercury

ROCK'S ULTIMATE SHOWMAN
5 SEPTEMBER 1946 – 24 NOVEMBER 1991

Freddie Mercury was Queen's flamboyant front man for two decades. He was the voice behind a string of worldwide hits, while his ermine-clad, coroneted entrances gave the regal seal to his majestic stagecraft.

Farrokh Bulsara was born in Zanzibar, where his father was a government accountant. He spent his early years in India, where he attended a boarding school near Mumbai, and also adopted the Freddie moniker. He took piano lessons and formed a band, but as he entered his teens, the family was on the move again. Concerned about the political climate, his Persian-born parents relocated to Feltham, Middlesex.

Brian May was a rising star, an accomplished guitarist in the bands 1984 and Smile. Bassist Tim Staffell played in both, while dental student Roger Taylor was recruited to play drums with Smile. It was Staffell who drew Mercury into the group's circle. Both attended Ealing College, where Freddie began a graphic art and

design course in 1966. Initially something of a hanger-on, Mercury opined that Smile needed more pizzazz. He had no doubts that he was a star in waiting, and that he could supply the panache Smile lacked. The group resisted his attempts to muscle in on the act, and in 1969 managed to secure a deal with Mercury Records when they were still a three-piece. Freddie responded by joining a northwest-based group – but they kept in touch. Freddie returned to the capital, Smile ran its course – dropped by Mercury – and Staffell departed.

Below: Queen pose in 1976: (L–R) Roger Taylor, Freddie Mercury, Brian May and John Deacon.

Opposite: Mercury performs at Live Aid, 1985.

Freddie at last officially hooked up with May and Taylor, with whom he'd run an art and fashion stall at Kensington market to make ends meet.

Freddie's propensity to camp it up with feather boas and painted nails raised few eyebrows. He had a steady girlfriend and his sexuality was not a topic for discussion when Queen – his choice of name for the new combo – took to the stage for the first time in 1970. This was the year that Freddie Bulsara became Freddie Mercury.

The loss of Staffell left an opening for a bass player. A couple came and went before John Deacon was recruited in February 1971. The line-up that would storm the charts was complete. Queen signed to EMI early in 1973, releasing their eponymous debut album and the May-penned single 'Keep Yourself Alive' the same year. Mercury's 'Seven Seas Of Rhye' gave them the first of their 19 UK Top 10 hits, culled from the *Queen II* album, which made the Top 5. All four were contributing to the writing, but it was Freddie's 'Killer Queen' that gave them their next singles success, peaking at No 2 in the United

'I always knew I was a star, and now the rest of the world seems to agree with me.'

Above: Brian May and Freddie Mercury interact on stage in Australia, 1985.

Right: Mercury with Mary Austin. Austin and Mercury were romantically linked during the 1970s and remained close friends throughout Mercury's life.

Opposite: Mercury sings in Chicago, 1980.

Kingdom. Parent album *Sheer Heart Attack* matched that chart performance, and both helped break the band in the United States.

Queen scaled new heights in 1975 with the release of Mercury's 'Bohemian Rhapsody'. EMI were nervous about putting out a seven-minute-long song with soaring operatic vocals. There was also a ground-breaking video, aired frequently as 'Bo-Rhap' dropped anchor at No 1 for nine weeks. The song featured on *A Night at the Opera*, which gave Queen their first album chart-topper.

Mercury went on to write 'Somebody to Love', the anthemic 'We Are the Champions', 'Don't Stop Me Now', and added rhythm guitar to his credits on 'Crazy Little Thing Called Love'. In 1981 he performed before a record 130,000 crowd in São Paulo, Brazil, and duetted with Bowie on 'Under Pressure', another No 1 hit. For many, Queen's set was the highlight of the 1985 Live Aid concert, Mercury at his strutting best. They gave their final live show at Knebworth the following year.

Freddie reinvented himself in the 1980s, mustachioed, cropped-haired and more muscular. He released his first solo single in 1984, and enjoyed his biggest successes away from Queen with 'The Great Pretender' and his duet with Montserrat Caballe, 'Barcelona', both of which made the UK Top 10.

On the private front, Mercury developed a cocaine habit, and having split with his girlfriend pursued a promiscuous gay lifestyle over many years. He was diagnosed as suffering from AIDS in 1987. Freddie grew a beard and used thick make-up to try to hide the ravages of the disease, but when he appeared in the video for 'I Want It All' in 1989, there was a tell-tale gauntness that increased speculation. The official announcement regarding his illness came just 24 hours before his death. 'These Are the Days of Our Lives', one of Mercury's final recordings, was released a month later, backed by 'Bohemian Rhapsody'. It went to No 1 and won a British Phonographic Industry award as the year's best single. 1995 saw the release of *Made in Heaven*, an album featuring material Mercury recorded during the latter stages of his illness. The spin-off singles included 'A Winter's Tale', the singer's final composition.

Keith Moon

LEGENDARY DRUMMER
23 AUGUST 1946 – 7 SEPTEMBER 1978

Keith Moon was the exuberant drummer of The Who; with his eccentric personality he became the epitome of the flamboyant side of rock 'n' roll. His lifestyle was based around excessive drinking, drug abuse and partying – so he also came to stand for rock's self-destructive tendencies.

Born Keith John Moon in London, Moon began his musical career playing the bugle and trumpet at Sea Cadets but at 13 moved to the bass drum. In 1961 he bought his first drums, a pearl-blue Premier kit, and began practising on his own as well as taking lessons from drummer Carlo Little of Screaming Lord Sutch and the Savages. Moon first became drummer for London band The Beachcombers, but at 17 left to join The Who.

Moon was such an intense drummer that his kit was secured on stage with rope. He played with a wild abandon that many would describe as lunatic, and at the culmination of live sets he and guitarist Pete Townshend initially destroyed their equipment in various elaborate ways – which brought the press attention they wanted. Moon provided the core of The Who's sound, making them distinct from other rock bands. He was a perpetual joker, making the others laugh during recording sessions – to the point where he was banned from the studio – and taking delight in dressing up,

'I told people I was a drummer before I even had a set, I was a mental drummer.'

stripping off or arriving in an unconventional manner. He also had a propensity for trashing hotel rooms, throwing TV sets through windows and blowing up toilets with explosives, which led to The Who being banned from most hotel chains around the world. One legendary tale involves a car being driven into a swimming pool – but is probably apocryphal.

Although his outrageous lifestyle often over-shadowed his talent, Moon is considered one of the great rock 'n' roll drummers; he produced dramatic and fluid drum rolls, combined with wild crashes on the cymbals and fast two-handed double bass drumming. He also sang – particularly at live performances – and was credited with composing several songs. He only released one album of his own, *Two Sides of the Moon*, which was not taken seriously on release but is now regarded as illustrating the essence of his talent. However, his chaotic lifestyle soon took its toll; on tour in 1973 he passed out on stage after ingesting a massive mixture of tranquillizers and alcohol. Moon finally died from an overdose of sedative prescribed to alleviate alcohol withdrawal symptoms as he tried desperately to get clean.

Top: (L–R) Roger Daltrey, John Entwistle, Keith Moon and Pete Townshend in 1970.

Right: Moon and David Essex pose together during the filming of the movie That'll Be the Day *in 1973.*

Opposite: Keith Moon pictured in 1965.

ICONIC ROCK STAR
8 DECEMBER 1943 – 3 JULY 1971

The Doors' lead singer Jim Morrison is still widely regarded as the definitive rock star: sexy, scandalous and often surly. As a lyricist he has become one of the most influential writers in rock history, with The Doors' songs still a staple of classic rock airtime.

James Douglas Morrison was born in Florida, although since his father was in the US Navy the Morrison family had a typical military nomadic life. The young Morrison was highly intelligent and, despite a routinely disrupted education, he developed an interest in literature, poetry and philosophy, particularly the works of Jack Kerouac, Friedrich Nietzsche, William Blake, Charles Baudelaire and French symbolist poet Arthur Rimbaud. After graduating from UCLA film school in 1965 Morrison cut off contact with his

family and began following a laid-back existence in Venice Beach, writing song lyrics and taking LSD. With Ray Manzarek, a friend from UCLA, he also formed The Doors; Morrison came up with the name after reading Aldous Huxley's account of drug experiences, *The Doors of Perception (1954)*.

The Doors, with their mixture of blues and rock, quickly became the first popular 'new wave' band. Their debut album, *The Doors*, released in 1967, was No 1 in the US, though it only just scraped into the British charts. The following albums, *Strange Days* and *Waiting for the Sun*, provided further US hits and, in 'Hello I Love You', a UK No 15. But by the end of 1969 Morrison's behaviour, fuelled by drink and drugs, was becoming more outrageous – he frequently arrived late or drunk and was arrested for 'indecent exposure, lewd conduct and public intoxication' after trying to start a riot during a concert in Miami. Although some charges were later dropped, the scandal made it hard for the band to perform live afterwards. Morrison put on weight and grew a beard, but the time out seemed to spur his creativity; one of the group's most critically acclaimed albums, *Morrison Hotel*, was released in 1970.

In spring 1971 Morrison relocated to Paris; he told several reporters that he wanted to drop music to become a writer. His long-term companion, Pamela Courson – whom he met before becoming famous – was with him in Paris and encouraged him to work on

'There are things known and things unknown and in between are the doors.'

Right: Jim Morrison and girlfriend Pamela Courson pictured in the Hollywood Hills, 1969.

Below: The Doors: Jim Morrison (vocals), Ray Manzarek (organ), Robby Krieger (guitar) and John Densmore (drums).

Opposite: Jim Morrison pictured in Los Angeles, 1968.

his poetry. However, within four months Morrison was dead after an apparently accidental overdose. His grave in Paris has become a shrine for successive generations of fans and since his death his records have never been out of print.

The Notorious B.I.G.

HIP-HOP RAPPING LEGEND
21 MAY 1972 – 9 MARCH 1997

One of the all-time great rappers, The Notorious B.I.G. had a wonderful ability to tell a complex story in a vivid and easy-to-understand way. During his lifetime his talent was sometimes overshadowed by his feud with former associate Tupac Shakur, which expanded to involve their record companies, Bad Boy and Death Row, and ultimately became the focus of a bitter East Coast/West Coast rivalry.

'I never wish death on nobody, 'cause there ain't coming back from that.'

Christopher Wallace was born in Brooklyn, New York; his father left early on but his mother was a schoolteacher, so the family was not as poor as Wallace later claimed. He began rapping as a teenager but by 1989 had dropped out of school and become involved in crime, later serving a short prison sentence for dealing drugs. After his release he made a demo, which found its way to Uptown Records in early 1992. Producer Sean Combs initially signed Wallace to Uptown, but when he started his own label, Bad Boy Records, he took Wallace along. Wallace planned to use his nickname, Biggie Smalls – he was over 6 ft tall and weighed over 20 stone – as his stage name, but it was already taken so he settled on The Notorious B.I.G.

Top left: The Notorious B.I.G. and Sean Combs at the Shrine Auditorium in Los Angeles in 1997.

Above: Performing at Meadowlands, New Jersey, in 1995.

Opposite: The Notorious B.I.G. was noted for his dark semi-autobiographical lyrics and storytelling abilities.

In 1994 B.I.G. released his first solo record, 'Juicy'/'Unbelievable', which reached the Top 30 and was followed by 'Ready to Die', which did even better, reaching No 13 in the US charts. At the time these were full of West Coast hip-hop, and B.I.G. was the artist who turned interest back towards the East. The following year he won several major awards, but also became involved in a public argument with Tupac Shakur, who accused him of being involved in an attack in 1994 in which Shakur had been shot and robbed. When Shakur signed with Death Row Records, the argument found a wider stage and quickly escalated into East versus West Coast.

In 1996 Shakur was shot and killed in Las Vegas; B.I.G. was an immediate suspect although he was recording in New York at the time. The following year B.I.G. was leaving a party in Los Angeles when his car stopped at a red light. Another car pulled up alongside, bullets were fired and B.I.G. was dead; his murder remains unsolved. He left only two albums released during his lifetime and two more recorded for release after his death, but he has come to be regarded as one of the greatest hip-hop rappers.

Gram Parsons

COSMIC COUNTRY ROCKER
5 NOVEMBER 1946 – 19 SEPTEMBER 1973

A cult figure while alive, Gram Parsons never found the wider fame he deserved. He pioneered the concept of rock bands playing country music and, although he sold few records, his work became enormously influential with other musicians such as The Rolling Stones, Emmylou Harris and Elvis Costello.

Parsons was born Cecil Ingram Connor III in Winterhaven, Florida; his mother, Avis, was the daughter of a Florida citrus magnate and his father, 'Coon Dog' Connor, was a famous World War II flying veteran. Despite wealth and privilege home life was unhappy – both his mother and father were alcoholics and Avis was also depressive. When Parsons was 12 his father committed suicide and two years later his mother married Robert Parsons, who adopted Gram and his sister Avis; Cecil Ingram Connor became Gram Parsons.

Parsons played with several bands while still at high school, including rock 'n' roll band The Pacers, folk group The Legends – with Jim Stafford and Kent Lavoie who later found fame as Lobo – and Shiloh, also folk-orientated. The day he graduated from high school, his mother died from alcohol poisoning. Afterwards Parsons briefly attended Harvard to study theology, but formed the International Submarine Band and then dropped

out of university and moved to New York to develop his country-influenced rock 'n' roll sound. In Los Angeles the band recorded a debut album, *Safe at Home*, but by the time it was released they had disbanded.

> *'I just don't like the label "country rock" … It's music. Either it's good or it's bad.'*

Top left: The influential Parsons created what he called 'Cosmic American Music'.

Above: The Flying Burrito Brothers with bassist Chris Ethridge and pedal steel player Sneaky Pete Kleinow pictured in 1969.

Opposite: Parsons emerged from a wealthy but troubled childhood to attend Harvard University.

In 1968 Parsons joined The Byrds and was influential on *Sweetheart of the Rodeo*, their only country album and a classic today. He left The Byrds after a few months and formed the Flying Burrito Brothers, with whom he recorded *Gilded Palace of Sin*. The album sold few copies, but brought Parsons a dedicated following of other musicians. In 1970 Parsons left the band and hung out with The Rolling Stones during recording of *Exile on Main Street*, while at the same time ingesting massive amounts of drugs and alcohol. In 1972 he met Emmylou Harris, who did the harmonies on his first solo album, *GP*. Following its release, Parsons toured the United States and recorded a second album, *Grievous Angel*, but in 1973 – while on holiday in his favourite place, Joshua Tree, California – he died after overdosing on tequila and morphine. He was to have been buried in New Orleans, but road manager Phil Kaufman stole the body and burned it in the Joshua Tree National Park, fulfilling a pact made with Parsons.

Elvis
Presley

THE KING
8 JANUARY 1935 – 16 AUGUST 1977

John Lennon spoke for countless teenagers the world over when he said 'nothing really affected me until I heard Elvis'. Bill Haley and others might lay claim to be the founding father of rock and roll, but it was Elvis who 'permanently changed the face of American popular culture', as US president Jimmy Carter put it after learning of his death. The word 'American' is somewhat redundant in that eulogy.

Elvis was the elder of twins born to Vernon and Gladys Presley in Tupelo, Mississippi, on 8 January 1935. His brother didn't survive, which no doubt helped form a special bond between mother and son. Indeed, it was a gift for Gladys that prompted 18-year-old Elvis to visit Sun Records in 1953. He paid $4 to record a version of 'My Happiness' – a dollar less than the prize money he'd won in a song contest a decade earlier. The

intervening years had been unremarkable. Elvis sang at the Pentecostal church the family attended, and taught himself the rudiments of guitar. The Presleys had moved to Memphis, where Elvis completed his education. Something of an outsider at school, he didn't do well academically and was driving a truck for a living when he went to Sun studios to cut the disc for his mother. Manager Marion Keisker was impressed enough to recommend him to Sun owner Sam Phillips.

Phillips didn't instantly concur, but heard enough to warrant recruiting guitarist Scotty Moore and bass player Bill Black and allowing the three to rehearse. It was during a break from a ballad they were working on that the combo began jamming 'That's All Right Mama',

Top: Elvis plays Vince Everett in Jailhouse Rock, *1957.*

Right: Elvis swivels his hips on The Milton Berle Show, *1956.*

Opposite: Presley's first RCA single 'Heartbreak Hotel', released in January 1956, was a No 1 hit.

and Phillips now knew he had found something unique: a white singer who sounded like a black artist. It became Elvis's debut single, the switchboard of the local radio station lighting up when it was aired. The reaction was the same when Elvis took to the stage, his smouldering looks, curled lip and overtly sexual strutting in themselves enough to elicit frenzied screams.

It was a localized phenomenon until late 1955, when Colonel Tom Parker arrived on the scene and assumed management control. He immediately negotiated a move to RCA, and when Elvis's first release for the new label, 'Heartbreak Hotel', rocketed to the top of the charts and stayed there for eight weeks, it made the $35,000 pay-off to Sun look like the steal of the century.

His gyrations were deemed too provocative for a mainstream audience, and he was filmed only from the waist up when he appeared on the *Ed Sullivan Show*. If parents were outraged by Elvis the Pelvis, the kids were beside themselves for a very different reason.

'Rhythm is something you either have or don't have, but when you have it, you have it all over.'

Above: Elvis and Ann-Margret in Viva Las Vegas, *1964.*

Right: Dressed in black leather, Elvis performs in the hugely successful 1968 Comeback Special.

Opposite: Elvis and Priscilla on their wedding day, 1 May 1967.

Elvis's third RCA release, the double-A-side 'Hound Dog'/'Don't Be Cruel' became the best-selling single of all time, its 11-week run at the top of the *Billboard* chart unmatched for over 30 years. 'All Shook Up' – his first UK chart-topper – and 'Love Me Tender' were among the crop of early hits, the latter also the title of his first film. The Lieber-Stoller-penned title track of his third movie, *Jailhouse Rock*, was another monster success, the first single to go straight to No 1 in the United Kingdom. Even his two-year spell on military service was exploited, the shaven-haired, uniformed Presley cutting a dash in *GI Blues*. It was while serving in West Germany that he met 14-year-old Priscilla Beaulieu, step-daughter of a US Air Force captain, whom he would marry in 1967. Daughter Lisa Marie was born in 1968, her parents divorcing five years later.

After returning to Civvy Street, Elvis swapped the raw edge of the early recordings for more middle-of-the-road crooning. Songs such as 'It's Now or Never' – a revamp of a 19th-century operatic classic – and 'Are You Lonesome Tonight?', an old Jolson number, were big hits, though unlikely to give parents apoplexy. The Beatles happened, and Britain became the epicentre of a new pop explosion. Meanwhile, the formulaic films continued, with diminishing returns setting in. A 1968 TV special put Elvis back on top, and the following year he played his first live show for eight years in Las Vegas,

the start of a hugely successful run on the cabaret circuit. In 1969 'Suspicious Minds' gave him his first US No 1 for seven years; it was also his last. The flamboyant jumpsuits revealed an increasing weight problem, and Elvis was taking a multitude of prescription drugs as well as bingeing on cheeseburgers. He needed hospital treatment on a number of occasions before suffering heart failure at his Graceland home on 16 August 1977. It isn't every day that political leaders comment on the passing of a pop star, but Elvis Presley – The King of Rock 'n' Roll – was much more than that. As President Carter noted: 'His death deprives the country of a part of itself.'

Otis Redding

KING OF SOUL
9 SEPTEMBER 1941 – 10 DECEMBER 1967

One of the most influential soul singers of the 1960s, Otis Redding symbolizes the power of pure Southern 'deep soul'. A self-professed country boy from Macon, Georgia, he had a powerful, deep voice, and an enormous natural talent for songwriting and arranging.

When Redding began his career in the early 1960s he styled himself as a singer on Little Richard, who also came from Macon. Gradually he found his own unique sound, giving both ballads and up-tempo songs an unusual syncopated rhythm. In 1962, while

recording material at Stax Records in Memphis as singer for Johnny Jenkins and The Pinetoppers, Redding took the opportunity to record a ballad he had written, 'These Arms of Mine', at the end of a session. After it became a hit his solo career was on its way and over the next few years songs such as 'I've Been Loving You Too Long', 'I Can't Turn You Loose', a cover of The Rolling Stones' song 'Satisfaction', and 'Respect' were all big sellers, although only one reached the Top 10.

When appearing in concert Redding often included ad libs in the lyrics or false endings and could quickly whip up excitement with the intensity of his performance. At the end of his show-stopping rendition of 'Try a Little Tenderness' at the Monterey International Pop Festival in June 1967, the audience demanded four encores. Monterey marked a major breakthrough to a wider set of fans, as the young and mainly white audience enthusiastically took him into their hearts. It appeared that Redding was poised on the brink of superstardom.

> ## 'If it takes music to get the attention of these young people, then let's educate them through music.'

Almost exactly six months later, Redding was dead – killed in a plane crash on his way to a concert in Wisconsin, along with most of his band, the Bar-Kays. Perhaps his most famous song was recorded just four days before his death; '(Sittin' On) The Dock of the Bay' was released in January 1968 and became Redding's first No 1 hit, staying at the top spot for four weeks. The song was reportedly unfinished; the whistling at the end was originally there to indicate that there were more words to come. There was enough unreleased material from the last recording sessions to create three more albums. In 2007 Redding's widow, Zelma, established a foundation in her husband's name to motivate young people to stay in education through programmes of music and the arts – a goal that she said had originally been her husband's dream.

Above: Otis Redding gives his all onstage in 1967.

Left: Otis Redding, Jim Stewart, Rufus Thomas, Booker T. Jones and Carla Thomas pose for a portrait after recording the hit 'Tramp' at Stax Records in Memphis, circa 1967.

Opposite: A publicity picture dating from the 1960s.

Tupac Shakur

INFLUENTIAL RAPPER
16 JUNE 1971 – 13 SEPTEMBER 1996

The best-selling rap/hip-hop artist ever, having sold nearly 80 million albums worldwide, Tupac Shakur was also a poet and actor. His raps tackled social issues, such as injustice, inequality, poverty and city life – as well as commenting on his feuds with other rappers – and were usually controversial, but also often offered hope.

Although he was born in East Harlem, New York, Tupac Amaru Shakur moved to Marin City, California, as a teenager and quickly became drawn into the West Coast vibe. He began to rap at an early age, starting Strictly Dope with Ray Luv and DJ Dize and later becoming a back-up dancer for alternative rap group Digital Underground. In 1991 his debut album, *2Pacalypse Now*, was critically acclaimed – but also drew criticism for the views it expressed of the police force. Over the next few years Shakur often found himself in conflict with the law, either through his actions or because of the influence of his music.

'I'm a reflection of the community.'

In 1994 Shakur was on trial for sexually assaulting a woman but the day before the guilty verdict he was shot five times in the lobby of a recording studio in Manhattan. The Notorious B.I.G. was working at the studio at the time, and Shakur came to believe that his former associate had something to do with the attack. After serving roughly a quarter of his sexual assault sentence, Shakur was bailed by Marion Knight of Death Row Records, in return for signing with the label – and the argument between Shakur and B.I.G. quickly became an East Coast versus West Coast feud.

Towards the end of the 1990s Shakur was planning to move into writing and directing films, and had started his own production company, Euphanasia. He planned to stage concerts that would be free to students with good grades, and was becoming involved with projects

Left: Tupac Shakur and MC Hammer attend the annual American Music Awards in 1996.

Opposite: Shakur pictured on stage in Chicago in 1994.

to build community and sports centres for inner-city kids. He was also working on a project that he hoped would bring the East/West Coast conflict to an end.

In September 1996 Shakur attended the Tyson–Seldon boxing match at the MGM Grand in Las Vegas. After leaving the match his car stopped at an intersection; within minutes he was the victim of a drive-by shooting and he died six days later in hospital. He had released five albums while alive, and left enough pre-recorded material for many more. Since his death, his work has influenced many other artists, including Eminem and 50 Cent.

Ritchie Valens

FIRST LATINO ROCKER
13 MAY 1941 – 3 FEBRUARY 1959

Despite his very brief career, Ritchie Valens left a lasting impact on rock 'n' roll with 'La Bamba', a high-energy reworking of a traditional Mexican *huapango*, sung entirely in Spanish. Valens put a new spin on it, adding garage-rock riffing and a raw, enthusiastic solo, in the process inventing Latino rock and creating a two-minute rock 'n' roll classic.

Ricardo Esteban Valenzuela Reyes was born in Pacoima, Los Angeles, and grew up surrounded by both traditional Mexican music and black R & B vocal groups. At nine he was given his first guitar and soon displayed considerable talent at playing, singing and songwriting. In 1956 he joined dance band The Silhouettes and was heard by Bob Keane, president of Del-Fi Records, who signed him to a recording contract, shortened his name to Valens and added the 't' to Richie. Valens's debut single, the original composition 'Come On, Let's Go', sold 750,000 copies and led to a short US tour. Back

Above: A rock 'n' roll pioneer, Valens's recording career lasted only eight months.

Right: Valens with Bob Keane, president of Del-Fi Records.

Opposite: Valens poses for his famous album cover session in July 1958, Los Angeles.

in the studio he recorded a song written for his high-school sweetheart, Donna Ludwig; 'Donna' became the A-side of his next release in October 1958, with 'La Bamba' on the B-side. 'Donna', a classic teen love ballad, reached No 2 in the charts – it was only later that 'La Bamba' became the more famous song, with its rapid guitar work and the thick sound of the relatively new 'electric' bass.

> ## 'My dreams are pure rock and roll.'
>
> *From La Bamba*

In January 1959, Ritchie was booked for the ill-fated 'Winter Dance Party' tour, with Buddy Holly and J. P. 'The Big Bopper' Richardson. During a gruelling series of one-night stands the tour bus developed heating problems and Holly's drummer was soon hospitalized

with frostbite. After a performance in Iowa they were all cold and tired so Buddy chartered a small plane to take himself and back-up musicians Waylon Jennings and Tommy Allsup to the next gig in Minnesota. Jennings gave his seat to Richardson, who was running a fever, and Valens flipped a coin with Allsup to win his seat. The single-engine aircraft took off in a blinding snowstorm but just minutes after take-off plunged into the ground killing all on board. Valens left a small but influential collection of recorded material and his legend grew in the years following his death, culminating in the 1987 film *La Bamba*, a dramatized version of his brief life and stardom. At the same time Hispanic-American group Los Lobos recorded their own version of 'La Bamba', which topped the US charts.

Sid Vicious

PUNK ROCKER
10 MAY 1957 – 2 FEBRUARY 1979

Although he was bass player of punk rock band the Sex Pistols, Sid Vicious couldn't play well – he was hired for his charisma and iconic punk image rather than for musicianship. Initially he tried to learn, but being a Sex Pistol soon became more about outrageous behaviour and scandal than about music, as the band lived up to its public image.

Born John Simon Ritchie in Lewisham, London, Vicious later became John Beverley after his mother remarried. At art college he met John Lydon (aka Johnny Rotten), who renamed him Sid Vicious, partly after Syd Barrett (ex-Pink Floyd guitarist) and partly after his hamster, Sid; the animal had bitten his friend, who exclaimed, 'Sid is really vicious!' The two Johns were living in a squat with others who had musical ambitions, and Vicious became part of several bands. Both boys also frequented Vivienne Westwood's shop in the Kings Road, and when Malcolm McLaren began managing the Swankers and was looking for a lead singer, Westwood suggested he try the boy called John who came into the shop. She meant Vicious, but McClaren approached Rotten and signed him as frontman for the newly-named Sex Pistols. However, when the original bass player left in 1977 Vicious took his place. Unexpectedly, the Sex Pistols captured the feelings of young people in the 1970s – punk was a means of self-expression and creativity, a call to stop complaining and take action.

'I'll die before I'm 25, and when I do I'll have lived the way I wanted to.'

Above: The Sex Pistols at the Longhorn Ballroom, Dallas, during their final tour in January 1978: (L–R) Sid Vicious, Steve Jones, John Lydon (aka Johnny Rotten).

Top right: Sid and his girlfriend Nancy Spungen in 1978.

Opposite: Sid Vicious at the Sex Pistols' last concert, San Francisco, California, January 1978.

Unfortunately, being part of all this had a destructive effect on Vicious; those who knew him said previously he was shy and a bit of a loner.

Later in 1977 Vicious met Nancy Spungen, a drug addict and groupie from New York. She is credited with introducing him to heroin; later Rotten said, 'We did everything to get rid of Nancy... I was absolutely convinced this girl was on a slow suicide mission... Only she didn't want to go alone. She wanted to take Sid with her.' But Vicious was besotted and when the Sex Pistols finally disintegrated during their 1978 US tour, he went solo with Spungen as his 'manager'. In October 1978 he woke to find her dead; she had been stabbed and he was arrested for murder, although by February 1979 he was out on bail. During a celebration party he overdosed on heroin and by the following morning was dead – later his mother found what she believed was a suicide note in his pocket.

Amy Winehouse

POP'S SOULFUL WILD CHILD
14 SEPTEMBER 1983 – 23 JULY 2011

After taking the pop world by storm with her 2006 album *Back to Black*, Amy Winehouse made headlines more for her alcohol and drug addictions than her soul-baring music.

Amy Winehouse grew up in north London, where she fell under the spell of jazz legends, such as Sarah Vaughan and Billie Holiday. A natural performer, she won a place at the prestigious Sylvia Young Theatre School, but her nonconformist streak meant she didn't stay the course. She fared better in the more relaxed atmosphere of the BRIT School, where she honed her guitar-playing and songwriting skills.

When Amy was 16, a demo tape circulated by her friend, singer Tyler James, led to a management deal with a company owned by Simon Fuller. A contract with Island Records followed. Her 2003 debut album, *Frank*, was well received, Winehouse winning an Ivor Novello award for the single 'Stronger Than Me'. The set also included 'F*** Me Pumps', a scabrous sideswipe at women on the make, and 'I Heard Love is Blind', which takes a wry look at infidelity. The hallmarks of searingly honest lyrics served up with raw intensity were already in place.

Three years passed before the release of *Back to Black*, an album inspired by her break-up with boyfriend Blake Fielder-Civil. He returned to a former love, as the bereft Amy describes movingly in the title track. Co-produced by Mark Ronson, the album had a 1960s soul feel, underscored by the singer's distinctive beehive hair and kohl-shrouded eyes. She mixed forthrightness, defiance and vulnerability in songs such as 'Rehab' and 'Love Is a Losing Game', the former chronicling an attempt by her manager to get her to seek help for her addictions. He went, the addictions stayed.

'I'm not here to be famous, I just want to challenge myself. If it all goes wrong, I'll have my music.'

Winehouse collected five Grammys for *Back to Black*, which topped the UK charts and debuted in the United States at No 7, an unprecedented achievement for a British female artist.

Fame and fortune couldn't halt the downward slide, nor could reconciliation with Fielder-Civil, whom she married in 2007 and divorced two tempestuous years later. She suffered dramatic weight loss, often appeared on stage intoxicated and a number of shows were cancelled. Shortly before she was found dead at her Camden home, a European tour was curtailed when she was clearly in no fit state to perform.

With her long-awaited third album still in development, Amy Winehouse left a small body of work, a clutch of songs with streetwise, heartfelt lyrics packing an emotional punch and delivered in her inimitable smoky vocal style.

Left: Amy poses with husband Blake Fielder-Civil in 2007.

Top: Amy with her father Mitch Winehouse pictured in 2010.

Opposite: Winehouse performs at the Riverside Studios during the 50th Grammy Awards ceremony in February 2008.

Frank Zappa

ECCENTRIC GENIUS
21 DECEMBER 1940 – 4 DECEMBER 1993

Frank Vincent Zappa was a prolific workaholic who was not only a brilliant rock guitarist, but also an orchestral composer, innovative film-maker and record producer, businessman, and forthright critic of education, religion, politics and censorship.

Born in Baltimore, Maryland, Zappa began playing drums at 12, but by 18 had switched to guitar. A self-taught musician, his tastes were wide ranging – he was interested in sound rather than a particular genre and quickly developed an innovative style. He dropped out of college after one term and began composing and playing music, as well as both writing and producing songs for other musicians. By the mid-1960s he was divorced from first wife, Kay, but had a recording studio with facilities to

'I never set out to be weird. It was always other people who called me weird.'

experiment with multi-track recordings, still unusual at the time. In 1965 he was entrapped by the local vice squad into making an alleged pornographic tape, which led to a brief stint in prison and the loss of the studio and much of his work – an event that hardened his anti-establishment stance. By 1966 Zappa was leading local band The Mothers, soon rechristened The Mothers of Invention, and began to release a series of groundbreaking records, such as 'Freak Out' and 'We're Only in it for the Money'. The lyrics of Zappa's songs often upset religious and political groups; he was an outspoken advocate of free speech.

Under his own name, Zappa released the influential jazz-rock fusion album *Hot Rats*, featuring a memorable vocal from Don Van Vliet, aka Captain Beefheart. Throughout the 1970s he released instrumental albums featuring orchestral music, jazz, his own guitar improvisations, and later synthesizers and sequencers. He also released vocal albums that, like his live concerts, specialized in jaw-dropping displays of technical virtuosity.

Zappa suffered from poor health in childhood, and in December 1971 was pushed off stage by a member of the audience and fell into the orchestra pit, suffering major fractures and a crushed larynx. He spent six months in a wheelchair and afterwards had a limp. In 1990 he was diagnosed with cancer; it had spread too far to operate. Before his death he was recognized as a composer of serious music when he featured at the 1992 Frankfurt Festival; the Berlin Ensemble Modern played *Shark Suite*, with two concerts conducted by Zappa himself. After Zappa died, his widow Gail, whom he had married in 1967, released a statement that simply stated: 'Composer Frank Zappa left for his final tour just before 6 pm Saturday.'

Top: Frank Zappa with his wife Gail and daughter Moon Unit in February 1968, Los Angeles.

Right: Zappa is regarded as one of the most original guitarists and composers of his time and wrote the lyrics to all his songs.

Opposite: Frank Zappa poses for a portrait in Rome, 1988.

Politicians & Activists

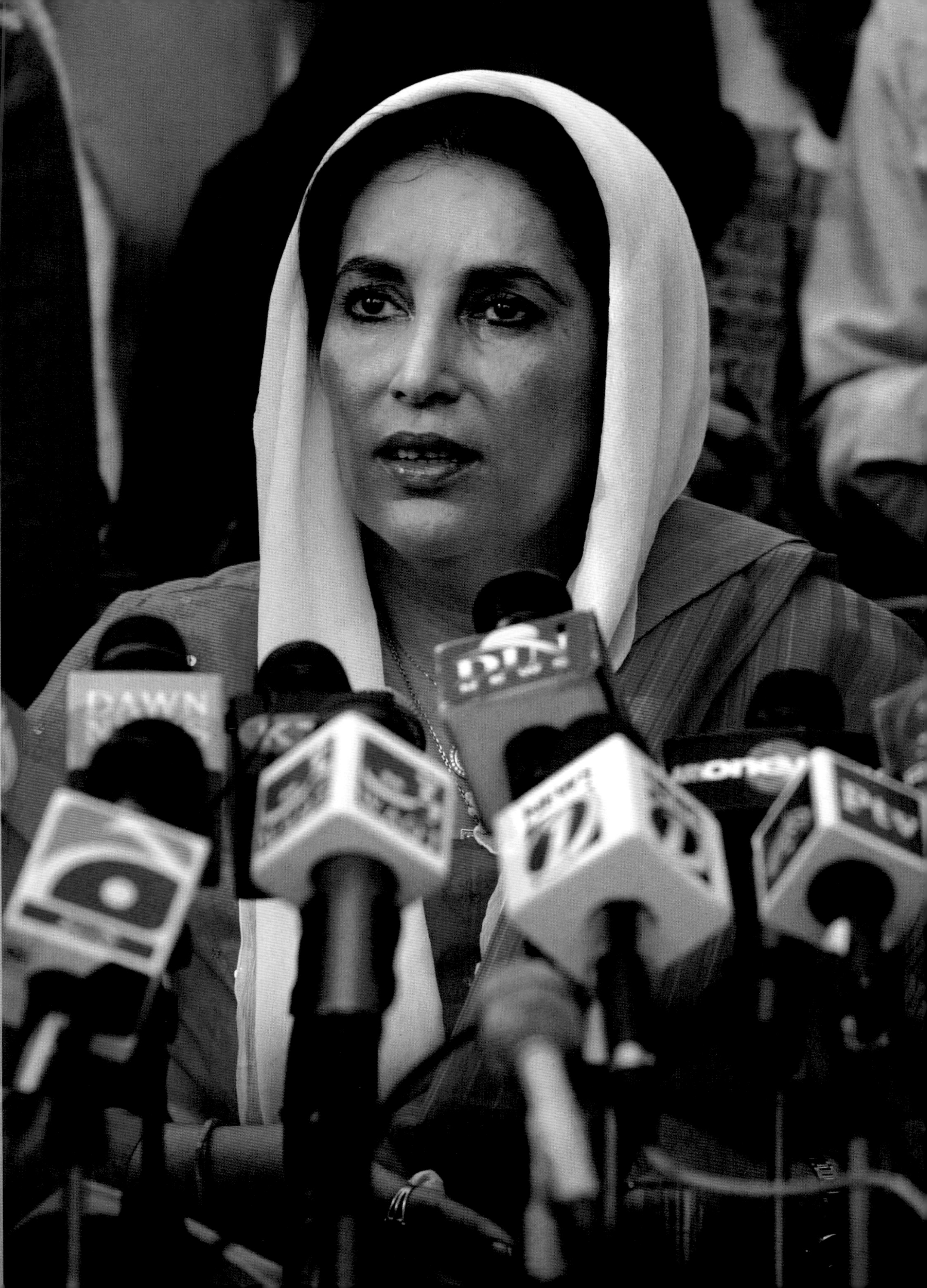
DAWN

Benazir Bhutto

FIRST WOMAN TO LEAD A MUSLIM NATION
21 JUNE 1953 – 27 DECEMBER 2007

Benazir Bhutto followed in her father's footsteps in becoming Pakistan's elected leader. Her reforming zeal made her many enemies and she was assassinated while campaigning for a third term in office.

Benazir Bhutto was born in Karachi, the daughter of a wealthy landowner and political activist who founded the Pakistan People's Party in 1967. She had a privileged upbringing, studying at Harvard and Oxford, where she was president of the Union. Her father, Zulfikar Ali Bhutto, led a democratically elected civilian government from 1971 to 1977, when he was ousted – and subsequently executed – in a military coup led by General Zia ul-Haq.

Benazir was incarcerated for five years and then spent a lengthy period in exile. Based in London from 1984, Bhutto entered into an arranged marriage in 1987, an idea she had come round to. Following Zia's death in 1988, Bhutto led the PPP to victory, promising to deliver economic, social and political reform. At 35 she became one of the youngest chief executives of a major nation, and the first female prime minister in an Islamic country.

Bhutto's first spell as Pakistan's premier ended in 1990, when she was dismissed over corruption charges. She returned to power in 1993, instituting a programme to improve education, housing and health care. As a moderate and a modernizer, Bhutto made many enemies. She said of Al-Qaeda, whom she believed to be behind more than one assassination attempt: 'I represent everything they fear the most – moderation, democracy, equality for women, information and technology.'

Bhutto was again forced out of power in 1996, refuting the corruption charges levelled against her and her husband Asif Zadari. He would spend eight years behind bars, while Bhutto left the country in 1998, the year before General Pervez Musharraf seized power. Musharraf was a weakened figure by 2007 and Bhutto,

now protected from past allegations by an amnesty, saw her opportunity 'to make Pakistan a positive model to one billion Muslims around the world'. The threat from radical Islamists was realized almost as soon as she set foot on home soil, Bhutto surviving a suicide bombing that claimed scores of lives. Her luck ran out two months later when she fell victim to an assassin's bullet after attending a rally in Rawalpindi.

> '**Despite threats of death, I will not acquiesce to tyranny, but rather lead the fight against it.**'

Right: Prime Minister Bhutto accompanied by President Bill Clinton at the White House, 1995.

Opposite: Benazir Bhutto speaks to the media in Lahore after being released from a period of house arrest following her return to Pakistan, November 2007.

Steve Biko

ANTI-APARTHEID MARTYR
18 DECEMBER 1946 – 12 SEPTEMBER 1977

Steve Biko was a political activist and leading light in the Black Consciousness movement during apartheid-era South Africa. He became a revered figure to those fighting the country's oppressive regime following his death while in police custody.

Born in King William's Town, Cape Province, Stephen Bantu Biko showed his rebellious colours at an early age when he was expelled from school for anti-establishment agitating. He went on to study medicine at the segregated Natal University, making his political mark in 1969 by founding the all-black South African Students' Organization. His motivation was the failure of the existing white-dominated national student body to address the needs of its black members.

Biko developed his ideas on Black Consciousness, a state of mind embracing 'group pride and the determination of the blacks to rise and attain the envisaged self'. The demand for integration was not enough; black people had to abandon feelings of inferiority as a prerequisite to empowerment. 'The most potent weapon in the hands of the oppressor,' he argued, 'is the mind of the oppressed.' Biko had in mind all non-whites suffering under apartheid, including Coloured and Indian citizens.

In 1972 Biko presided over the Black People's Convention, an umbrella body for black organizations, which struggled in the face of state repression. The following year he was issued with a banning order that imposed severe restrictions on his freedom of movement and speech. Even so, his pronouncements were instrumental in igniting the 1976 student-led Soweto riots, which broke out over the statutory delivery of the curriculum in Afrikaans – regarded as the linguistic symbol of a reviled regime.

Biko was arrested four times, detained without trial for long periods. The last such occasion was 18 August 1977, when he was jailed in Port Elizabeth. He died in Pretoria Central Prison 25 days later, the most prominent fatality while in police custody but by no means the only such death. Scorn was immediately poured on the official version of events, that Biko was a hunger-strike victim, and the inquest revealed that he died from a brain haemorrhage. Twenty years would pass before five ex-police officers admitted to administering beatings that resulted in his fatal injuries. By then apartheid had been consigned to the history books, realizing Biko's dream 'to bestow upon South Africa the greatest gift possible – a more human face'.

> ' We have set out on a quest for true humanity and somewhere on the distant horizon we can see the glittering prize.'

Opposite: Steve Biko, whose story was brought to a huge international audience by journalist Donald Woods's book Cry Freedom, *which was made into a feature film of the same name.*

Right: Thousands attend Steve Biko's funeral in King William's Town, September 1977.

Che Guevara

REVOLUTIONARY LEADER
14 JUNE 1928 – 9 OCTOBER 1967

Che Guevara had a privileged upbringing in his native Argentina, training as a physician before becoming a professional revolutionary and poster boy for the 1960s student protest movement.

Ernesto Guevara was born in Rosario, Argentina, a sickly, studious child whose ambition was to aid humanity by studying medicine. Guevara qualified as a doctor in 1953, but his extensive travels throughout South and Latin America radically changed his perspective. He witnessed widespread deprivation, and was also on hand to see the left-wing government of Guatemala overthrown in a US-backed coup in 1954. He determined to become a 'revolutionary doctor', but realized that an individual contribution in his chosen field was a worthless, if noble, pursuit. There could be no love between master and slave; the destruction of that relationship was a precondition for love to blossom. Revolutionizing the system, he posited, necessitated a revolution.

Guevara met a number of Cuban exiles on his travels, and it was they who gave him his nickname,

from his own habit of using 'che' as a greeting – 'pal' in his native patois. He met law graduate Fidel Castro in Mexico in 1955, the latter already having served time in a Cuban jail for attempting to incite a people's revolt in that country. He joined Castro's revolutionary '26th of July Movement' and was part of an 80-strong force that landed in Cuba in 1956 with the aim of unseating the corrupt government led by General Fulgencio Batista. Clashes with government soldiers reduced the guerrilla force to just a handful of men, among them Guevara. This small contingent established a base in the Sierra Maestra, from where it began its long armed

Opposite: A classic image of Che Guevara with a lit cigar clenched between his teeth, 1959.

Below: Guevara appears on the CBS current affairs programme Face the Nation, *14 December 1964.*

Above: Che Guevara smokes cigars with ABC news correspondent Lisa Howard, circa 1960.

struggle. Guevara became Castro's trusted lieutenant, one whose 'resolute contempt for danger' helped ensure the fight continued even when the odds were unfavourable. Guevara would write a handbook on how to wage guerrilla warfare, knowledge accumulated over a two-year campaign. At first the rebels worked to win

> 'The revolution is not an apple that falls when it is ripe. You have to make it fall.'

over the impoverished, distributing hard-won territory among the peasant population. The middle classes were converted as Batista's forces used brutal methods to discourage people from joining the rebellion. Many demoralized government soldiers allied themselves with the insurrection, and even though Batista enjoyed American logistical support, the tide became unstoppable. Batista fled the country, and Castro assumed control in January 1959.

Guevara took Cuban citizenship, was put in charge of the National Bank and set about implementing economic reforms, which met with limited success.

He also showed his ruthless credentials as head of La Cabaña prison in Havana, said to have been responsible for dispensing summary justice to hundreds of enemies of the new regime. In 1961 he was appointed Minister for Industries, but even as a senior apparatchik he never departed from his battle fatigues. That endeared him to the world's youth, a symbol for those who were becoming politicized and questioning the established order. The iconic photograph of Guevara, which would adorn countless bedroom walls, was taken by Alberto Korda, who had worked at the fashion end of the market in pre-revolutionary Cuba. Ironically, he didn't think it worthy of publication at the time, the picture remaining in his private collection for several years. In 1967, the year of Guevara's death, he gifted a print to an Italian publisher, who made a fortune distributing the image of a man for whom material gain was anathema.

Guevara believed that revolution was something that could be successfully exported to other countries where people suffered grinding poverty under an oppressive regime. He spoke of wanting to make the Andes the Sierra Maestra of that continent. In a letter to Castro in 1965 he wrote: 'I have fulfilled the part of my duty that bound me to the revolution in your territory. I formally resign from my post as major, as minister, and my status as a Cuban.' He also spoke of his 'obligation to fight against imperialism wherever it may be'. Castro produced this document in October 1965 to explain Guevara's disappearance from public life over recent months. The latter had made some strident anti-Soviet noises, and as it wasn't in Cuba's interest to ruffle Moscow's feathers, some concluded that it was a timely parting of the ways.

After visiting the Congo, Vietnam and his homeland, Guevara set down in Bolivia, where he began to foment rebellion. He led guerrilla raids, but became frustrated by the lack of progress. Ill health was also an impediment. Guevara had suffered from asthma since childhood, and was plagued by mosquito bites, to which he reacted badly. His physical condition may have caused him to drop his guard while trying to recruit tin-miners living in straitened circumstances. He was captured and executed by the Bolivian army, his death serving only to enhance his status as a romantic idealist, martyr to a cause he selflessly embraced, champion of the downtrodden and dispossessed.

Top: Ernesto Che Guevara, wearing military fatigues, listens to proceedings with a headset at the United Nations, 12 December 1964.

Right: Fidel Castro, Prime Minister of the Cuban Revolutionary government and first secretary of the Cuban Communist Party, and Che Guevara, Minister of Industries, pictured during a popular meeting in Havana, circa 1960.

John F. Kennedy

KING OF CAMELOT
29 MAY 1917 – 22 NOVEMBER 1963

When John F. Kennedy won the 1960 presidential election, becoming the 35th incumbent of that office, for millions of Americans it marked a new dawn of hope and optimism. There was a buoyant mood abroad that went far beyond the sanguinity that greets most new administrations.

Kennedy was the first White House occupant to be born in the 20th century and the youngest elected president, he had charisma, vitality and film-star looks. He and his wife Jacqueline brought glamour to the highest office in the land, lending an air of enchantment to the Camelot court over which they presided. John Fitzgerald Kennedy was born in Brookline, Massachusetts, the second son of Boston-Irish Catholics Joe and Rose Kennedy. It was a privileged upbringing. His father was a wealthy businessman, a philanderer and a politician himself – appointed ambassador to Britain in the 1930s. The family was steeped in the Democratic Party traditions of a city that had become a stronghold for that political hue following the transatlantic influx during the 19th century. The Kennedys were high achievers, and when the first-born son, Joe Jr, was killed in the war, Jack was anointed as the one for whom great things were planned and expected. He was praised for his analysis of British foreign policy in the run-up to World War II in *Why England Slept*, published in 1940, the year he graduated from Harvard. Military service followed, Kennedy adding war hero to his curriculum vitae for leading the surviving crew members to safety after his torpedo boat was sunk by a Japanese warship.

He was elected to the House of Representatives in 1946, and to the Senate six years later. In 1953 the rising political star married Jacqueline Bouvier, whose beauty and sophistication made her a fashion icon. They would have three children, Caroline, John and Patrick, who died at only a few days old . While recovering from one of several back operations, Kennedy wrote *Profiles In Courage*, which brought him a Pulitzer Prize. He missed out on being Adlai Stevenson's running mate in the 1956 presidential election, which was seen as a blessing in disguise as Eisenhower was returned to office. Kennedy raised his profile while remaining untainted by defeat.

Four years later, Kennedy triumphed narrowly over Richard Nixon, becoming the first Catholic to be voted into the White House. This was the first election played out on television, and in the broadcast debates the telegenic Kennedy scored heavily over his jowly, sweat-browed rival. In his inaugural address he stirred the nation with rousing oratory, urging Americans to 'ask not what your country can do for you; ask what you can do for your country'. Kennedy's New Frontier

Above: John F. Kennedy and his younger brother Robert F. Kennedy pictured together in 1960.

Opposite: Kennedy makes a point during a campaign speech in Illinois, 1960.

Above: Portrait of the Kennedy family at Brookline, Massachusetts, 1930s. Front row (L–R): Joseph P. Kennedy Jr, Rose Kennedy, Robert Kennedy, Edward Kennedy, Joseph P. Kennedy Sr, Patricia Kennedy, Jean Kennedy; back row (L–R): Eunice Kennedy, John F. Kennedy, Kathleen Kennedy and Rosemary Kennedy.

Left: Kennedy walks alongside his bride Jacqueline Bouvier at an outdoor reception, Newport, Rhode Island, 1953.

programme embraced education, health and civil rights, though a number of measures stalled in Congress and it was left to his successor Lyndon Johnson to implement many key social reforms. Another target he didn't live to see realized was putting a man on the moon before the decade was out. The space race with the Soviet Union was running at the height of the Cold War.

In 1961 Kennedy suffered a humiliating reverse in the Bay of Pigs incident, a CIA-backed plan to unseat Fidel Castro, the Marxist Cuban leader who had gained power in 1959. A year later, he faced down Nikita Khrushchev over Russia's attempt to establish missile bases on Cuba, the closest East and West have come to nuclear conflagration. Kennedy's belief in

with the signing of a nuclear test ban treaty, albeit one limited in scope.

On 22 November 1963 Kennedy visited Texas to deal with Democratic Party in-fighting, clearing the path towards the 1964 presidential election and a bid for a second term. He suffered fatal bullet wounds as his open-top limousine made its way through central Dallas. Ex-marine Lee Harvey Oswald, who had once defected to the Soviet Union, was soon in police custody. He was an employee of the Texas Book Depository overlooking Dealey Plaza, from where the shots had been fired. Two days later the putative assassin was himself shot and killed by nightclub owner Jack Ruby. After a year-long investigation, the Warren Commission concluded that Oswald was the lone gunman. It didn't prevent speculation that other dark forces were at work that day, from Cuban hit men to the Mafia. Conspiracy theories have abounded ever since, all predicated on the notion that Oswald was the 'patsy' he claimed to be.

Left: President John F. Kennedy makes the State of the Union Address in 1962 as Vice President Lyndon Johnson looks on.

Below: The Kennedys arrive at Love Field near Dallas on the day of his assassination, 22 November 1963.

'And so, my fellow Americans, ask not what your country can do for you; ask what you can do for your country.'

the domino theory underpinned his support for South Vietnam, regarded as a bulwark against the spread of Communism in Southeast Asia. Once again, it was a policy that would play out in the years after his death. In June 1963 he reassured the people of West Berlin, a divided city since 1961, that an attack on their freedom was an attack on liberty itself. 'All free men,' he declaimed from the city hall balcony, 'wherever they may live, are citizens of Berlin, and, therefore, as a free man, I take pride in the words: *Ich bin ein Berliner.*' Relations between the superpowers thawed somewhat

Robert F. Kennedy

STATESMAN IN A POLITICAL DYNASTY
20 NOVEMBER 1925 – 6 JUNE 1968

Robert Kennedy orchestrated the campaign that carried his elder brother to the White House in 1960. Eight years later, he was on the verge of securing the Democratic Party's presidential nomination when he, too, was struck down by an assassin's bullet.

Robert Francis Kennedy was born in Brookline, Massachusetts, the seventh of Joseph and Rose Kennedy's nine children. His father was a wealthy businessman, his mother the daughter of a long-serving Boston mayor. Robert was steeped in the family credo of endeavour and competitiveness, where high achievement was expected. Political ambition was also ingrained. His father served as ambassador to Britain; his eldest brother was marked out for high office before he was killed in World War II; and he ran the campaign that installed the second-born son, John F. Kennedy, in the White House.

> ## 'Only those who dare to fail greatly can ever achieve greatly.'

A Harvard-educated law graduate, Robert also worked in the Department of Justice in the 1950s. He was chief counsel to the Senate Committee on Improper Practices from 1957–59, making his mark in his relentless pursuit of notorious Teamsters Union boss Jimmy Hoffa.

His reward for helping steer his brother to the presidency was the post of Attorney General, which afforded him the opportunity to continue the fight against union racketeering and organized crime. He also took on big business, ordering an investigation into the steel industry. Civil rights was also a key policy issue. Kennedy implemented the 1954 Supreme Court ruling on school desegregation, and deployed federal troops to ensure that southern states toed the non-discriminatory line. His role was much broader, though; he was a key advisor to the president in all policy areas.

Kennedy resigned as Attorney General shortly after JFK's death, choosing to advance his career as senator for New York when President Lyndon B. Johnson made it clear he didn't want him as running mate at the 1964 election. His supporters saw Johnson as a usurper, and there was little love lost between the two men. Kennedy criticized Johnson's handling of the Vietnam War, pledging to end the conflict, while showing his liberal colours on domestic issues.

Below: Kennedy poses at his desk during his stint as Attorney General, 1962.

Opposite: Robert Kennedy meets the press in London, 1967.

He announced his bid for the White House in March 1968, staying his hand until Senator Eugene McCarthy entered the race and exposed Johnson's vulnerability. Robert Kennedy received fatal gunshot wounds at the Ambassador Hotel, Los Angeles, having just secured victory in the key California primary. His assassin, Sirhan Sirhan, was a Jerusalem-born Palestinian who opposed Kennedy's support for Israel, the shooting taking place on the first anniversary of the Six-Day War.

Martin Luther King Jr.

CIVIL RIGHTS CHAMPION
15 JANUARY 1929 – 4 APRIL 1968

With his inspirational oratory and unswerving adherence to the principles of peaceful protest, Martin Luther King pricked America's conscience on the civil rights issue. He ignored threats to his personal safety to lead the fight for equality, a struggle 'to save the soul of America'.

Martin Luther King was born in Atlanta, Georgia, the son of a Baptist minister. He followed in his father's footsteps after studying at a seminary, then gaining a doctorate at Boston University in 1955. He became pastor of Dexter Avenue Baptist Church in Montgomery, Alabama, and soon found himself at the eye of a political storm. In December 1955, African-American seamstress Rosa Parks was arrested after refusing to give up her seat in the whites-only section of the bus on which she was travelling. It became one of the great causes célèbres of the civil rights movement, and King was thrust into the limelight as leader of the subsequent year-long boycott of bus companies operating a discriminatory service. He was a great admirer of Mahatma Gandhi, who had waged a long, non-violent campaign for India's independence. Using economic leverage to drive home a political point sat well with that philosophy. To Gandhi's approach he bolted on the Christian tenets of love and forgiveness, qualities he would need in abundance over the next decade, not least when he was jailed, received death threats and had his home bombed. Gandhi had a well-defined opponent in an imperial overlord; King had to contend with fear and deep-rooted prejudice.

The Supreme Court outlawed the discriminatory practices on Alabama's buses in 1956, the first of a number of legislative victories during King's time at the forefront of the civil rights movement. It soon became apparent that changes in the law weren't enough. In 1957 state troops were deployed in Little Rock, Arkansas, to prevent black students from taking their places at the desegregated high school. It was one of a number of face-offs between southern state leaders and the Federal Government, demonstrating that it was necessary to win hearts and minds as well as legal battles.

King resigned his pastorship in 1960 to focus solely on the civil rights issue. There was a pressing need to channel mounting student unrest, ensuring that the

Top: Martin Luther King and his wife, Coretta Scott King, emerge from Montgomery Court House, following his trial on charges of conspiring to boycott segregated city buses, 23 March 1956.

Right: The Reverend King testifies during a racial trial in Florida, 1963.

Opposite: Reverend Martin Luther King relaxes at home in Montgomery, Alabama, 1956.

principle of non-violent protest was maintained. There were those keen to adopt a more militant stance who accused King of being a latter-day Uncle Tom.

In 1961 he began the 'Freedom Rides', which eventually brought an end to segregation on inter-state travel. Two years later, he organized a Freedom March on Washington. He spoke movingly about a 'promissory note' that the country's founding fathers had signed, one that America had defaulted on in its treatment of black people. With the chiding came a vision of a better future. 'I have a dream that my four little children will one day live in a nation where they will not be judged by the colour of their skin but by the content of their character.' It was a 'promised land' King said he himself might not reach. That was a prescient remark, for changing attitudes was a glacially slow business, and he was under constant threat from hard-liners wedded to the old order.

President John F. Kennedy introduced a Civil Rights Bill that became law in 1964, after his assassination. King was awarded the Nobel Peace Prize the same year. The Voting Rights Act was passed in 1965, but the struggle was far from over. Every success provoked a backlash from reactionaries. Speaking in Atlanta in 1967, King said: 'Discrimination is a hellhound that gnaws at Negroes in every waking moment of their lives, to remind them that the lie of their inferiority is accepted as truth in the society dominating them.'

'Injustice anywhere is a threat to justice everywhere.'

By 1968 swathes of the population were still disadvantaged in areas such as employment and housing. King launched the Poor People's Campaign, attacking poverty afflicting all strata of society. His hope was for an 'Economic Bill of Rights' to be introduced, a campaign still in its infancy when King was shot while standing on the balcony of his Memphis hotel room on 4 April 1968. James Earl Ray was arrested in London two months later. He pleaded guilty and received a life sentence, though he later changed his story, protesting his innocence right up to his death in 1998.

Martin Luther King is revered for his work in the field of human rights, an inspiring figure whose oft-quoted words have lost none of their impact as a battle cry for equality and indictment of injustice. Numerous posthumous honours were conferred on him, statues erected, streets named in his honour; and on the third Monday in January each year America celebrates the life and achievements of one of its greatest sons on Martin Luther King Day.

Opposite: Martin Luther King waves to supporters from the steps of the Lincoln Memorial on 28 August 1963 during the 'March on Washington' at which he made the famous 'I Have a Dream' speech.

Below: King marches with hundreds of supporters and members of the Chicago Freedom Movement along State Street, Chicago, Illinois, 26 July 1965.

Harvey Milk

COURAGEOUS EQUAL RIGHTS CAMPAIGNER
22 MAY 1930 – 27 NOVEMBER 1978

Harvey Milk knew he was putting himself in the firing line, literally as well as metaphorically, when he successfully ran for office in San Francisco in 1977. The city's first openly gay elected official, Milk said his achievement offered 'hope for a better tomorrow'.

Harvey Milk was a New Yorker by birth, his family running a retail business on Long Island. After high school he attended the New York State College for Teachers, graduating in 1951. Milk served in the US Navy in the Korean War, claiming his sexuality lay behind his 1955 discharge, though his version of events does not accord with the official record. A mathematics major, he used his skills as an insurance actuary, and later as a financial analyst on Wall Street.

He was a successful banker, but the work held little interest for him.

In 1972 Milk moved to San Francisco, heart of the 1960s counterculture scene and home to America's largest gay community. He opened a camera shop, and in 1973 made his first bid to join the city's Board of Supervisors. Unlike some of his gay friends, who preferred to keep their heads below the parapet and try to effect change by stealth, Milk opted for the loud and proud approach. His boldness had a

'If I do a good job, people won't care if I am green or have three heads.'

Below: Mayor George Moscone and Supervisor Harvey Milk at a ribbon-cutting ceremony, San Francisco, 1978.

Opposite: Harvey Milk poses outside his camera shop after his 1977 election to the Board of Supervisors.

galvanizing effect. Supporters formed human billboards, outing themselves as they propelled Milk into office at the third attempt.

In his brief period as a supervisor, Milk took care to avoid being seen as a single-issue politician. He took up the dog-fouling problem with gusto, but knew that no amount of positive PR would change the minds of bigots who found his elevation unacceptable. He even made a tape recording anticipating his death, which came at the hands of ex-firefighter and former supervisor Dan White, a fervent opponent of the gay rights legislation that had been passed. The city's

mayor George Moscone was also shot and killed. Dan White's sympathetic hearing and lenient sentence prompted a violent backlash.

Milk himself had not wanted recriminations in the event of his death. 'If a bullet should enter my brain,' he said, 'let that bullet destroy every closet door.' It was an overly ambitious exhortation, of the kind one would expect from such an inspirational figure. Sean Penn, who gave an Oscar-winning performance in the 2008 biopic *Milk*, called him 'a great, beautiful, brave man'. In 2009 Harvey Milk was posthumously awarded the Presidential Medal of Freedom.

Eva Perón

FIRST LADY OF ARGENTINA
7 MAY 1919 – 26 JULY 1952

Eva Perón, popularly known as Evita, was the object of an almost mystical adoration by Argentina's people. Many regarded her as a saint, and the Vatican received thousands of requests for her official canonization in the two years following her death.

Maria Eva Ibarguren was born in rural Argentina, the daughter of a ranch manager and his mistress. Some sources give her birth surname as Duarte (her father's surname) but her parents were unmarried and illegitimacy often caused her to be treated unjustly as she grew up. A lively, intelligent girl, Evita left for Buenos Aires when she was a teenager to begin a career as an actress. After a few small film and stage parts she found regular work on radio and by 1943 was one of the highest paid actresses in the country.

In 1944 Evita became involved in a series of fund-raising events to help earthquake victims, and at the final gala she met the Secretary of Labour, a popular politician named Juan Perón. Within weeks, she was sharing his apartment. Perón went on to become Vice President of the Republic, but political unrest at the end of World War II led to his arrest and imprisonment in 1945, although he was quickly released after a populist revolt. Soon after his release Perón married Eva and the following year began campaigning for president. Evita supported him on the campaign trail – the first woman in Argentinian politics to do so – and although the upper classes disapproved of her

'I am only a simple woman who lives to serve Perón and my people.'

she quickly became increasingly popular with ordinary people, who gave her the nickname Evita.

After Perón was elected, Evita campaigned for labour rights and on behalf of votes for women; she was instrumental in the formation of the Perónist Women's Party. She also established the Eva Perón Foundation, which supported the poor in practical ways – donating goods or awarding scholarships, as well as building homes and hospitals. Evita herself worked at the Foundation every day, meeting those who came to ask for help in person. In 1951 she was put forward as vice-presidential candidate and despite opposition from the military she had overwhelming support from the general population. However, at the same time her health was

declining; she was subsequently diagnosed with cancer and died the following year. In a massive outpouring of grief, nearly a million Argentinians crowded the streets of Buenos Aires for her funeral procession.

Above: Juan and Eva Perón and Colonel Mercante read a newspaper together following Perón's election as president in February 1946.

Below: Eva Perón addresses a crowd of women in 1951.

Opposite: Eva Perón holds up her hands in a gesture of mild protest in 1947.

Malcolm X

BLACK NATIONALIST LEADER
19 MAY 1925 – 21 FEBRUARY 1965

Malcolm X was at the forefront of America's civil rights movement in the 1950s and 1960s. Initially, he pursued separatist goals and saw violence as an acceptable instrument of change, but later renounced his extreme views and advocated universal brotherhood.

He was born Malcolm Little in Omaha, Nebraska, the son of a Baptist minister who was targeted by the Ku Klux Klan for his outspoken campaigning on behalf of the Universal Negro Improvement Association. The family relocated to Lansing, Michigan, where, in 1931, Earl Little died in mysterious circumstances. The official line was that he fell into the path of a streetcar, a tragic accident. Others said he was pushed. His wife suffered a breakdown and had to be institutionalized.

'Sitting at the table doesn't make you a diner.'

Malcolm Little and his siblings were farmed out to assorted foster homes. A gifted student harbouring ambitions for a career in law, he went off the rails in his teens and was jailed for burglary in 1946. While in prison he embraced the teachings of Elijah Muhammad, a self-proclaimed messenger of Allah who rejected the integrationist objectives of many civil rights leaders, favouring instead the establishment of a separate state for African Americans. Little converted to Elijah Muhammad's Nation of Islam and became one of its chief spokesmen following his release from jail in 1952. He also swapped his 'slave name' for Malcolm X.

Vehemently opposed to the non-violent stance taken by Martin Luther King and his ilk, Malcolm X spoke of 'the irrelevance of integration for the black poor, and the self-loathing implied in begging for it'. He argued that in a battle between the empowered and dispossessed nothing would be achieved without revolution and bloodshed. His extreme views and inflammatory words – including the comment that Kennedy's assassination was a case of 'chickens coming home to roost' – made him a bogeyman to white

Left: World heavyweight boxing champion and Nation of Islam member Muhammad Ali is approached by Malcolm X in February 1964.

Opposite: Malcolm X makes a speech in March 1964.

America, and also eventually led to a rift with Elijah Muhammad. In 1964 he left the Black Muslims to found the Organization of Afro-American Unity, and began campaigning for racial harmony rather than separatism. By focusing on human rather than civil rights, he sought to bring an international dimension to the struggle for justice and equality. However, Malcolm X had made many enemies among his former associates, and the three men convicted of gunning him down during an OAAU meeting at New York's Audubon Ballroom on 21 February 1965 had known connections with the Black Muslims.

109

Actors

John Belushi

INVENTIVE, IRREVERENT, IRREPRESSIBLE COMEDIAN
24 JANUARY 1949 – 5 MARCH 1982

John Belushi's comic creations and manic impressions on the TV show *Saturday Night Live* made him a star, and he was much in demand when he turned his considerable talent to the big screen.

The son of Albanian immigrants, John Belushi grew up in Wheaton, Illinois. Football, playing the drums and acting were all high on his list of interests during his schooldays, but the last of those was top of the list. In 1971 he joined Chicago's famed Second City group, which launched many star careers. Aping the likes of Joe Cocker gave him the opportunity to go

wildly over the top, and Belushi established himself as a marvellous physical comedian.

In 1973 Belushi appeared in the off-Broadway production of *Lemmings*, a send-up of Woodstock-type festivals. The show was a spin-off from the *National Lampoon* magazine, and five years later Belushi would make his movie splash when the same publication took to the big screen with *Animal House*. He played beer-swilling slob Bluto Blutarsky in the hit college campus comedy that launched a long-running franchise.

By then *Saturday Night Live* had made him a household name. Belushi was a member of the 'not-ready-for-primetime' cast when the show launched in October 1975. Audiences lapped up his blues-loving Beethoven, his bee-suited antics and his samurai warrior deli service.

Belushi initially ran his TV and film careers in tandem, but from 1979 focused exclusively on movie projects. He and fellow SNL performer Dan Aykroyd appeared in Spielberg's misfiring comedy *1941*, the negative reception not extending to Belushi's Wild Bill Kelso, which one reviewer described as 'splendidly gross'. The two then starred in *The Blues Brothers* (1980), a slow-burning cult hit whose origins could be traced to the TV series.

There was a change of gear for *Continental Divide* (1981), Belushi taking the romantic lead as a newspaperman who falls for an eagle expert. That same year saw him sparring with Aykroyd again in *Neighbors*, Belushi playing against type as the mild-mannered guy having to deal with a loose cannon residing next door. By spring 1982, Aykroyd already had his friend and collaborator pencilled in for their next joint venture, the paranormal romp *Ghostbusters*. It was still on the drawing board when Belushi, a long-time drug-user, was found dead from an overdose in a Los Angeles hotel room. His supplier Cathy Smith served a 15-month jail term after admitting to injecting the cocktail that killed the 33-year-old actor.

'Some comedians love their characters. I don't fall in love with mine.'

Above: Belushi with fellow comedian Steve Martin, 1981.

Left: Dan Ackroyd and John Belushi as the Blues Brothers.

Opposite: Performing in Blues Brothers Live, Concord Pavilion, California, 1980.

John Candy

BEAR-SIZED FUNNYMAN
31 OCTOBER 1950 – 4 MARCH 1994

John Candy made his name as a stage and TV comic before establishing himself as a fine comedic screen actor. In an industry notorious for big egos, he was much admired for his generosity of spirit: a genial, gentle giant.

John Franklin Candy hailed from Toronto, showing talent on the football field during his high school days, as well as being bitten by the drama bug. The larger-than-life, avuncular persona that would be his screen trademark was already to the fore, and it served him well as he combined acting classes with journalism studies. Performing won out when it came to choosing a career path.

Unsurprisingly, he was a big hit with kids during a spell in a children's theatre group. TV and low-budget movie work followed, but it was his Emmy award-winning contributions to the Second City comedy group that gave his career a major boost. The sketch show, which featured improvised skits and showed off Candy's gift for mimicry, transferred successfully to the small screen.

Dan Aykroyd – a friend of Candy's since their teens – and John Belushi were among the other Second City graduates who carved out a successful film career, Candy appearing in their 1980 cult hit *The Blues Brothers*. The following year, he was one of the

> ## 'I think I may have become an actor to hide from myself. You can escape into a character.'

Below: Candy plays Lasky the guard in Harold Ramis's National Lampoon's Vacation *(1983).*

Opposite: John Candy photographed in 1993.

misfit recruits in the army comedy *Stripes*. After his breakthrough playing Tom Hanks's womanizing brother in *Splash* (1984), Candy went on to appear in a string of hit comedies, including the remake of *Brewster's Millions* (1985) and Mel Brooks's *Spaceballs* (1987).

He was a regular in John Hughes's films, memorable as the garrulous, well-meaning shower-curtain-ring salesman who blights Steve Martin's homeward journey in *Planes, Trains and Automobiles* in 1987. Two years later, he traded one-liners with Macaulay Culkin in *Uncle Buck*, playing the eponymous relative charged with taking responsibility for his brother's kids. It was classic Candy territory: peel away the slobbish exterior and a heart of gold is revealed.

Oliver Stone's *JFK* (1991) saw Candy in a dramatic role, and in the same year he trod similar ground to Ernest Borgnine's 'Marty' by playing an unlikely romantic lead, trying to woo Ally Sheedy in the face of an overbearing mother. The actor himself was married with two children.

John Candy was sensitive about his 20-stone frame, not least because his father had died young from heart disease. He was 43 when he suffered a fatal heart attack while filming *Wagons East!* (1994). The film was completed using a double and dedicated to his memory.

TROUBLED ACTOR
17 OCTOBER 1920 – 23 JULY 1966

Montgomery Clift excelled in plumbing emotional depths as he played troubled characters, often outsiders. Off-screen he was conflicted over his sexuality, and decline set in after a car accident left him with appalling injuries.

Born in Omaha, Nebraska, Montgomery Clift found his métier in his early teens, first in summer stock, then on Broadway. He spent over ten years on the New York stage, gaining a reputation as an actor of great intelligence and sensitivity. He was also strikingly handsome and an obvious target for Hollywood producers.

Clift turned 28 the year he made his big-screen debut, opposite John Wayne in the western *Red River* and in *The Search*, both released in 1948. The latter brought him the first of three Oscar nominations in five years. Those industry accolades were indicative of the fact that Clift was highly selective in his choice of projects.

A Place in the Sun (1951) and *From Here to Eternity* (1953) brought him further nods from the Academy. The former, which saw him as an ill-fated social climber, marked the first of a trio of pairings with Elizabeth Taylor, who would be a lifelong friend and confidante. 'She feels like the other half of me,' said Clift of the woman who saved his life in May 1956. It was while on his way home from a party at Taylor's home that he crashed his car, sustaining horrific facial injuries. Taylor was soon on the scene, helping him breathe by removing teeth implanted in the back of his throat. They were making the Civil War drama *Raintree County* together, director Edward Dmytryk using creative camera angles to hide the disfigurement.

'I'm just trying to be an actor; not a movie star, an actor.'

It wasn't the end of his career, but undoubtedly the start of a long decline in which drink and drugs took their toll. He would notch a fourth Oscar nomination for a cameo in *Judgment at Nuremberg* (1961), and took the lead in John Huston's biopic *Freud* (1962). Clift also shared the screen with Clark Gable and Marilyn Monroe in *The Misfits* (1961). Tellingly, Monroe said he was 'the only person I know who is in worse shape than I am'.

Taylor tried to revive his flagging career, offering to underwrite any losses when nervous backers baulked at the prospect of casting him in *Reflections in a Golden Eye*. The role of a repressed homosexual military man eventually went to Marlon Brando. By the time of its release, Clift had succumbed to a heart attack. His death was described by actor-director Robert Lewis, who had known him since his Broadway days, as 'the longest suicide in history'.

Opposite: A publicity still taken in the late 1940s, the beginning of Clift's Hollywood career.

Left: Posing with close friend Elizabeth Taylor, who saved his life in 1956.

Above: On the set of Raintree County *with Eva Marie Saint.*

James Dean

REBEL WITHOUT A CAUSE
8 FEBRUARY 1931 – 30 SEPTEMBER 1955

He starred in just three films, only one of which had been released when he met his end at the wheel of a Porsche Spyder. That narrow body of work was enough for James Dean to establish himself as an actor of rare talent, and as a cult figure among the angst-ridden teens of the rock 'n' roll generation.

James Byron Dean was born in Marion, Indiana, his dental-technician father moving the family to Los Angeles when he was five. The death of his mother when he was eight precipitated a return to the Midwest, Dean going to live with an aunt and uncle as his father struggled to cope as a single parent. Home was an Indiana farm during his high-school years, Dean proving to be an unexceptional student. The loss of his mother made him withdrawn and restless – feelings he would display so vividly on screen – though he did find an outlet in drama and sport. He determined on an acting career, to which end he returned to California after graduating from Fairmount High. There was a brief

reunion with his father, who by now had a new wife in tow. He briefly attended UCLA and augmented his studies at a drama workshop run by James Whitmore, who would enjoy an illustrious career as a character actor. Whitmore had helped found the Actors Studio, and it was he who introduced Dean to the Method approach and advised him to head to New York to hone his skills.

Below: Dean and director Nicholas Ray discuss a scene from Rebel Without a Cause *at the Griffith Park Observatory, LA.*

Opposite: James Dean sitting on his Porsche Speedster in Los Angeles, 1955.

A few bit-parts and commercials gave him the wherewithal to relocate to the East Coast in 1952. These included uncredited, blink-and-you-miss-him appearances in the war movie *Fixed Bayonets!*, the Dean Martin-Jerry Lewis vehicle *Sailor Beware* and *Has Anybody Seen My Gal*, in which his future *Giant* co-star Rock Hudson took the male lead.

Actors Studio guru Lee Strasberg recognized his potential, and over time Dean would inevitably be compared with Marlon Brando, a Method exponent who exploded onto the scene while Dean was scrabbling around for stage and TV work. His first Broadway play, *See the Jaguar*, bombed, but he got good notices for his performance in André Gide's *The Immoralist*. That won him a Daniel Blum Theater World award as one of the rising stars of 1954, a prize Brando himself had collected eight years before. It also secured him a screen test at Warner Brothers and a return to the movie-making capital, this time with stardom in his sights.

'Dream as if you'll live forever. Live as if you'll die today.'

Dean's star-making role was Cal Trask in the Elia Kazan-directed adaptation of Steinbeck's *East of Eden* (1955). His performance as the embittered son feeling unloved by patriarch Raymond Massey brought the first of two Oscar nominations, though Dean was dead before that peer recognition was bestowed upon him. His efforts weren't always appreciated by Massey, a distinguished, old-school actor who struggled with some of his young co-star's improvised emoting. Kazan didn't play peacemaker; he knew the creative tension would give their scenes added edge.

There was more familial dysfunctionality at the centre of Dean's next film, *Rebel Without a Cause* (1955), which put middle-class juvenile delinquency under the microscope. Dean played Jim Stark, 'a creature trying desperately to communicate his need and his loneliness', as one reviewer put it, adding: 'All that he

Left: James Dean chats with actress Pier Angeli, with whom he had a brief romance, in 1954.

Above: Dean poses on the set of the Warner Brothers' film East Of Eden *in 1954.*

Opposite: Pictured with co-star Elizabeth Taylor on the set of Giant *in 1956.*

can manage is a kind of inspired yet jerky, intermittent, uncertain form of Morse code.' He was the misfit who rails at his bickering parents: 'You're tearing me apart!'

Dean's final film, completed just before his death, was *Giant* (1956), a sprawling family saga based on an Edna Ferber novel. He played Jett Rink, an outsider and tortured soul once again, even after striking it rich in the oil business. Shooting had just finished when 24-year-old Dean headed for Salinas, California, in his silver Porsche to indulge his other great passion, motor racing. His contract put this thrill-seeking pastime off limits. Ironically, as a brief window of self-indulgence opened up, it was the journey to the start line that cost him his life. He was involved in a fatal head-on collision en route to the race. There was further irony in the fact that he had featured in a road-safety film in which he

highlighted the dangers of the highway compared to the track.

Rebel Without a Cause was released shortly after Dean's death. *Giant* followed a year later and brought him a second posthumous Best Actor nomination, an achievement unmatched in the 80-plus years since the awards were instituted.

The outpouring at Dean's death was similar to that which followed news of Rudolph Valentino's demise some 30 years earlier. Both had a brooding, smouldering appeal, but while Valentino was selling sex, Dean was the embodiment of misunderstood, rebellious youth. He has maintained that symbolic status ever since, connecting with generations of teens who have experienced the same concerns, frustrations and uncertainties Dean portrayed so astutely on screen.

Rainer Werner
Fassbinder

GERMAN CINEMA'S CONTROVERSIAL WUNDERKIND
31 MAY 1945 – 10 JUNE 1982

Director, actor, screenwriter and film editor, Rainer Werner Fassbinder was one of the leading lights of 1970s New German Cinema. A left-winger with a pessimistic world view, Fassbinder turned a cold eye on contemporary society.

Born in Bavaria as the dust was settling on the century's second global conflagration, Fassbinder had little contact with his doctor father after his parents separated when he was five. His mother was to become a member of his tight-knit company, a troupe that also included his ex-wives as well as male and female lovers. That working arrangement helped Fassbinder capture his vision on film with remarkable speed and efficiency, as did his single-take approach. He produced 41 films in just 13 years.

A movie fanatic from an early age, he said that Hollywood productions 'left the audience with emotions and nothing else'. Fassbinder wanted to give the viewer 'the possibility of reflecting on and analysing what he is feeling'. One mainstream director he admired was compatriot Douglas Sirk, whose 1950s melodramas dealt with strife lurking beneath superficial contentment. Fassbinder's *Fear Eats the Soul* (1974) was a remake of Sirk's *All That Heaven Allows*.

> **'Everyone must decide for himself whether it is better to have a brief but more intensely felt existence or to live a long and ordinary life.'**

Fassbinder saw parallels between 1970s Germany and the Weimar Republic, a right-wing trend he wanted to expose 'so that they won't just stupidly and unconsciously go along with it, like in the past'. He also believed the country's post-war economic miracle provided a veneer of fulfilment and false optimism. Entrapment was also a recurring theme. In *Why Does Herr R. Run Amok?* (1970) a seemingly successful man kills his family before taking his own life. *In Despair* (1978) a chocolatier plans to disappear by switching identities with a tramp.

At the time of his death from a drug overdose, Fassbinder had embarked on a series of films featuring female characters, whose stories were intended as a commentary on the body politic. *In The Marriage of Maria Braun* (1978), Fassbinder's most successful film, Hanna Schygulla stars in a tale of marital frustration that was an allegory of post-war Germany. The titular character in *Veronika Voss* (1982) is a morphine-dependent, has-been actress in the clutches of a doctor out to profit at the addicts' expense. The narcotics officers are in league with the pushers, personal decline echoed in a moribund state. Interviewed shortly before his death, Fassbinder said: 'Women are the social underdogs. It is sometimes easier to understand the oppressor by showing the behaviour of the oppressed and his – her – way of coping with it.'

Above: Italian actor Franco Nero, actress and singer Jeanne Moreau and actor Brad Davis on the set of Querelle *(1982).*

Opposite: Fassbinder pictured on the set of Despair *(1978).*

Judy Garland

'MISS SHOWBUSINESS'
10 JUNE 1922 – 22 JUNE 1969

Judy Garland shone brighter than any star during the golden age of screen musicals. Her talent was ruthlessly exploited, while her private life was a chaotic, drug- and alcohol-fuelled rollercoaster in which happiness was a fleeting commodity.

It's unlikely that Judy Garland remembered a time before she was a performer. She was born Frances Gumm to theatrical parents in Grand Rapids, Minnesota, taking to the stage at the age of three and later joining her mother and older sisters in a family act. As an ensemble it wasn't a great success, but the troupe's youngest member had clear potential, which her mother was determined to milk for all its worth.

Those efforts brought 13-year-old Frances a screen test at MGM and a seven-year contract. Having signed her, the studio didn't seem to know what to do with her. Garland was teamed with another young hopeful, Deanna Durbin, in the 1936 short *Every Sunday*, and legend has it that Louis B. Mayer was ready to drop her. In the event, she was loaned out to Fox to make the college musical *Pigskin Parade* (1936), appearing well down a bill that included Betty Grable.

Garland's cause was championed by MGM musical director Roger Edens, who recognized 'the biggest thing to happen to the MGM musical'. Mayer was struggling to see past the puppy fat, but came round after Garland sang a revamped version of 'You Made Me Love You' as a birthday tribute to MGM top dog Clark Gable. The number was worked into *Broadway Melody of 1938* (1937), and in the same year she made *Thoroughbreds Don't Cry*, a racetrack yarn that was the first of several pairings with Mickey Rooney.

Garland had quickly established herself as a headliner for routine pictures, but there were doubts as to whether she could carry a big-budget production, such as *The Wizard of Oz*. MGM's first choice, Shirley

Right: Seventeen-year-old Garland stars as Dorothy in The Wizard of Oz *(1939).*

Opposite: A studio portrait of the young Garland.

125

Temple, couldn't be prised from Fox, and the role of Dorothy fell to 17-year-old Judy. Her enchanting performance brought a special Oscar 'for her outstanding performance as a screen juvenile'. The 1939 film also provided Garland with her signature song, 'Over the Rainbow'.

A strict dieting regimen was imposed to control Garland's weight, and her routine soon included pep pills and sleeping tablets. When it was suggested by one health expert that she needed time away to help get off the chemical treadmill, a studio executive said it was impossible, as 'we have $14 million tied up in her'.

She had her first solo starring role in *For Me and My Gal* (1942), and two years later headed the cast of *Meet Me in St. Louis*. She initially resisted the latter, trying to break free from juvenile roles, yet it became one of MGM's best-loved musicals of the era. It also yielded 'The Trolley Song', another perennial favourite on the Garland play list. The film's director, Vincente Minnelli, later became the second of her five husbands, the union producing daughter Liza, who would add another Oscar to the family haul for her turn in *Cabaret (1972)*.

Above: Judy Garland and Mickey Rooney, who appeared together in a string of successful musicals, including three in the Andy Hardy series.

Below: Garland in the MGM musical Meet Me in St. Louis *(1944).*

remake of *A Star Is Born* (1954). It put her briefly back on top and brought a Best Actress nomination. That she lost out to Grace Kelly for *The Country Girl* was described by Groucho Marx as 'the biggest robbery since Brinks'. It was a blow that did nothing to help someone suffering suicidal bouts of depression. Garland missed out again for her straight-acting cameo in *Judgment at Nuremberg* (1961), this time in the supporting category. Her final screen appearance was also her first British film, *I Could Go on Singing (1963)*, an unworthy vehicle with which to sign off.

Judy Garland was found dead in her London flat on 22 June 1969, the coroner ruling that she had died from an accidental overdose. Ray Bolger, who played the Scarecrow in *The Wizard of Oz*, said the 47-year-old star 'just plain wore out'. Right up to her death she had been filling concert halls with her legions of devoted fans. One such, reviewing her performance in *The Times*, said: 'For a definition of theatrical magic one need look no further.'

'I was born at the age of 12 on an MGM lot.'

In 1948 she teamed up with Kelly again for *The Pirate*, and shared a screen for the first and only time with Fred Astaire in *Easter Parade*. The rot set in the following year when MGM took her off *The Barkleys of Broadway*, and she suffered a breakdown while making *Annie Get Your Gun* and again had to be replaced. She returned to make *Summer Stock* (1950) before her contract was terminated.

Garland turned to the stage, wowing audiences in London and New York with her concert performances. Those successes enabled third husband Sid Luft to negotiate a return to Hollywood for a Warner Brothers'

Above: Garland steps out with Fred Astaire in the 1948 musical Easter Parade.

Right: Garland and her daughter Liza Minnelli, who was born in 1946, pictured together in London in 1962.

Jean Harlow

PLATINUM BLONDE BOMBSHELL
3 MARCH 1911 – 7 JUNE 1937

Jean Harlow was a sex siren who inspired the famous line, 'Nobody ever starved possessing what she's got'. She was also a fine comedienne who had a string of box-office hits before her death at the age of 26.

Born into a well-to-do Kansas City family, Jean Harlow went to Hollywood in 1923, not to seek her fortune as a child star but to further the theatrical ambitions of a domineering, manipulative mother. Once it became clear that they would not be realized, 'Mama Jean' turned her attention to shaping a screen career for her daughter. It was she who decided on the blond rinse to mark her child out from the crowd.

In the late 1920s Harlow was a bit-part player contracted to Hal Roach, best known for his Laurel and Hardy productions. She made an impact in *Double Whoopee* (1929), in which she alights from a cab outside a hotel, only for bellhop Stan to trap her dress in the door, causing her to enter the building in a slip.

Harlow made her breakthrough playing a vamp in Howard Hughes's World War I epic *Hell's Angels (1930)*. A series of bad-girl roles followed, which played better with the public than the critics. One reviewer said her 'virtues as an actress are limited to her blonde beauty'. Such notices didn't stop men getting hot under the collar or women trying to copy her hair colour. The comedy *Platinum Blonde* (1931) was titled to promote her career, and the following year she joined MGM's roster.

Harlow regularly teamed up with Clark Gable, and it was while they were making *Red Dust* (1932) that her second husband, studio executive Paul Bern, was found dead from gunshot wounds. Suicide was the official verdict in a cause célèbre that remains shrouded in mystery.

'I like to wake up each morning feeling a new man.'

With films such as *Bombshell* (1933) and *Dinner at Eight* (1934), Harlow finally began to enjoy critical acclaim as well as box-office popularity. Her private life, however, was another matter. Marriage number three, to cameraman Hal Rosson, was soon on the rocks, and she never made it to the altar with William Powell, her co-star in the 1935 musical *Reckless* and the last great love of her life.

Jean Harlow died from uremic poisoning while making the racetrack drama *Saratoga* (1937), which was completed using body and voice doubles. Her mother, a Christian Science adherent, was said to have refused her the treatment that almost certainly would have saved her life.

Left: The blonde bombshell poses with her last great love, William Powell, circa 1935.

Above: All dressed up with Carl Randall in Reckless *(1935).*

Opposite: Jean Harlow as Lil Legendre in MGM's The Red-Headed Woman *(1932).*

Grace Kelly

HOLLYWOOD ROYALTY AND REAL-LIFE PRINCESS
12 NOVEMBER 1929 – 14 SEPTEMBER 1982

Grace Kelly was one of the great screen beauties, an Oscar-winning actress whose talent matched her exquisite looks. At 26 she left the stage to marry into one of Europe's oldest royal houses, a storyline worthy of Hollywood itself.

Grace Kelly came from well-heeled Philadelphian stock, the daughter of a successful businessman who was a gold-medal-winning Olympic rower. A beloved uncle, who was both an actor and playwright, provided inspiration, and after graduating Kelly struck out for New York to pursue her own theatrical ambitions. She studied at the American Academy of Dramatic Art,

> ## 'The idea of my life as a fairy tale is itself a fairy tale.'

supporting herself through modelling work and the odd TV advertisement.

Kelly made her Broadway debut opposite Raymond Massey in a production of Strindberg's *The Father*, which opened in November 1949 and ran for two months. She appeared in numerous live television dramas, and made her screen debut in the 1951 film *Fourteen Hours*, but her heart lay in theatre; she took the role merely to broaden her experience. The classic western *High Noon* (1952), in which she played Gary Cooper's Quaker bride, didn't alter that view. She signed up to *Mogambo* (1953) chiefly to work with Clark Gable and John Ford, with location shooting in Africa

Above: Kelly with James Stewart in Hitchcock's Rear Window.

Right: The world watched as Grace Kelly married Prince Rainier in Monaco in April 1956.

Opposite: Kelly, the epitome of elegance, pictured in 1955.

an added bonus. That brought a Supporting Actress Oscar nomination, and she took home a statuette the following year for her turn as the careworn wife to Bing Crosby's alcoholic singer in *The Country Girl*. The Oscar came in the middle of a trio of films she made with Alfred Hitchcock, Kelly becoming the latest in a long line of cool, elegant, blonde leading ladies favoured by the Master of Suspense.

She met Prince Rainier III of Monaco while attending the 1955 Cannes Film Festival, *Paris Match* brokering a meeting between one of the world's most eligible bachelors and a Hollywood glamour queen. They married a year later, after she'd signed off by playing Tracy Lord in *High Society*, her 11th film. Over the years there was much speculation that Her Serene Highness might make a 12th, especially after her three children had grown up. Narration and poetry recitals were the nearest she came to returning to her old profession until she appeared as herself in a comedy short just before her fatal car accident in 1982. Kelly suffered a stroke while at the wheel; daughter Stephanie survived the crash. The film, titled *Rearranged*, was mothballed after her death and never went on general release.

Heath Ledger

ACCLAIMED ACTOR
4 APRIL 1979 – 22 JANUARY 2008

Heath Ledger's breakthrough came in the 1999 teen rom-com *10 Things I Hate About You*, *The Taming of the Shrew* reworked for the American high-school scene. After scoring a big hit with what was his first US feature, he could have traded on his beefcake appeal. Instead he did the very opposite, seeking out challenging roles, sometimes involving physical transformations that masked his pin-up-boy looks.

Heathcliff Andrew Ledger grew up in Perth, Australia, his parents naming him after the brooding hero of *Wuthering Heights*. Bitten by the acting bug, the teenage Ledger worked his way into TV and films, including the popular soap *Home and Away* and *Sweat*. American audiences first saw him in the 1997 Fox TV series *Roar* but it was pulled from the schedules before all the episodes were aired, and two years went by before his Hollywood entrée. He played Mel Gibson's son, fighting to free America from the British yoke in *The Patriot* (2000). Billy Bob Thornton was his screen father in *Monster's Ball* (2001), the two united by their prison-officer jobs but little else. *A Knight's Tale* (2001) combined medieval jousting with a rock score, and the following year he played Harry Faversham in a remake of *The Four Feathers*.

> ## 'I only do this because I'm having fun. The day I stop having fun, I'll just walk away.'

After returning to his homeland to star in a retelling of the Ned Kelly story, Ledger hooked up with *A Knight's Tale* director Brian Helgeland again for the religious thriller *The Order* (2003). He co-starred with Matt Damon in Terry Gilliam's misfiring fantasy-drama *The Brothers Grimm* (2005), but was lauded for his portrayal of a tortured cowboy in *Brokeback Mountain (2005)*, married to Michelle Williams but drawn to Jake Gyllenhaal. He and Williams were both Oscar-nominated, and they began an off-screen romance that lasted until shortly before his death.

After taking on the roles of Casanova and Bob Dylan, Ledger gave an extraordinary performance as the Joker in Christopher Nolan's *The Dark Knight* (2008). 'Menacing, mercurial, droll and diabolical' was how

Kevin Kline summed it up on Oscars night, when Ledger was named Best Supporting Actor. His family collected the award, for Ledger was found dead in his New York apartment on 22 January 2008. Accidental overdose was the official verdict. The 28-year-old star, who wore fame and celebrity lightly, was working on Terry Gilliam's *The Imaginarium of Doctor Parnassus* when he died. It was completed by having his character transmute, allowing other actors to take on the role.

Above: On the set of Brokeback Mountain, *for which Ledger was Oscar-nominated for Best Actor in a Leading Role.*

Opposite: Ledger photographed in 2005.

Bruce Lee

HOLLYWOOD'S FIRST ASIAN SUPERSTAR
27 NOVEMBER 1940 – 20 JULY 1973

Bruce Lee's martial arts and acting skills made him one of the hottest big-screen action heroes of the early 1970s. He broke down barriers in becoming the first Asian actor to carry a big-budget Hollywood movie.

Bruce Lee crossed cultural boundaries from the moment he was born. He entered the world in San Francisco, where his father, a respected film and stage actor-singer, was on tour with the Cantonese Opera Company. His parents called him Lee Jun Fan, but it was a Western name, Bruce – a nurse's suggestion – that stuck.

The family was soon back in Hong Kong, where the boisterous, energetic Bruce spent his childhood years. With a father in the theatrical business, he was used to being around film sets, and was soon appearing in front of the cameras. Lee was a natural performer but he had an arrogant, pugnacious streak that landed him in many scrapes in a city where street gangs were rife. After taking one heavy beating, Lee took up martial arts, studying under renowned master Yip Man. He proved himself an able student of the physical aspects of Wing Chun, but his appreciation of the spiritual side of the discipline was lacking. After one brawl too many, 18-year-old Bruce was sent off to America.

Below: Bruce Lee and American actor Van Williams, who starred together in the TV series The Green Hornet, *circa 1966.*

Opposite A publicity still for Enter the Dragon (1973) *shows Lee with scratches across his chest and face.*

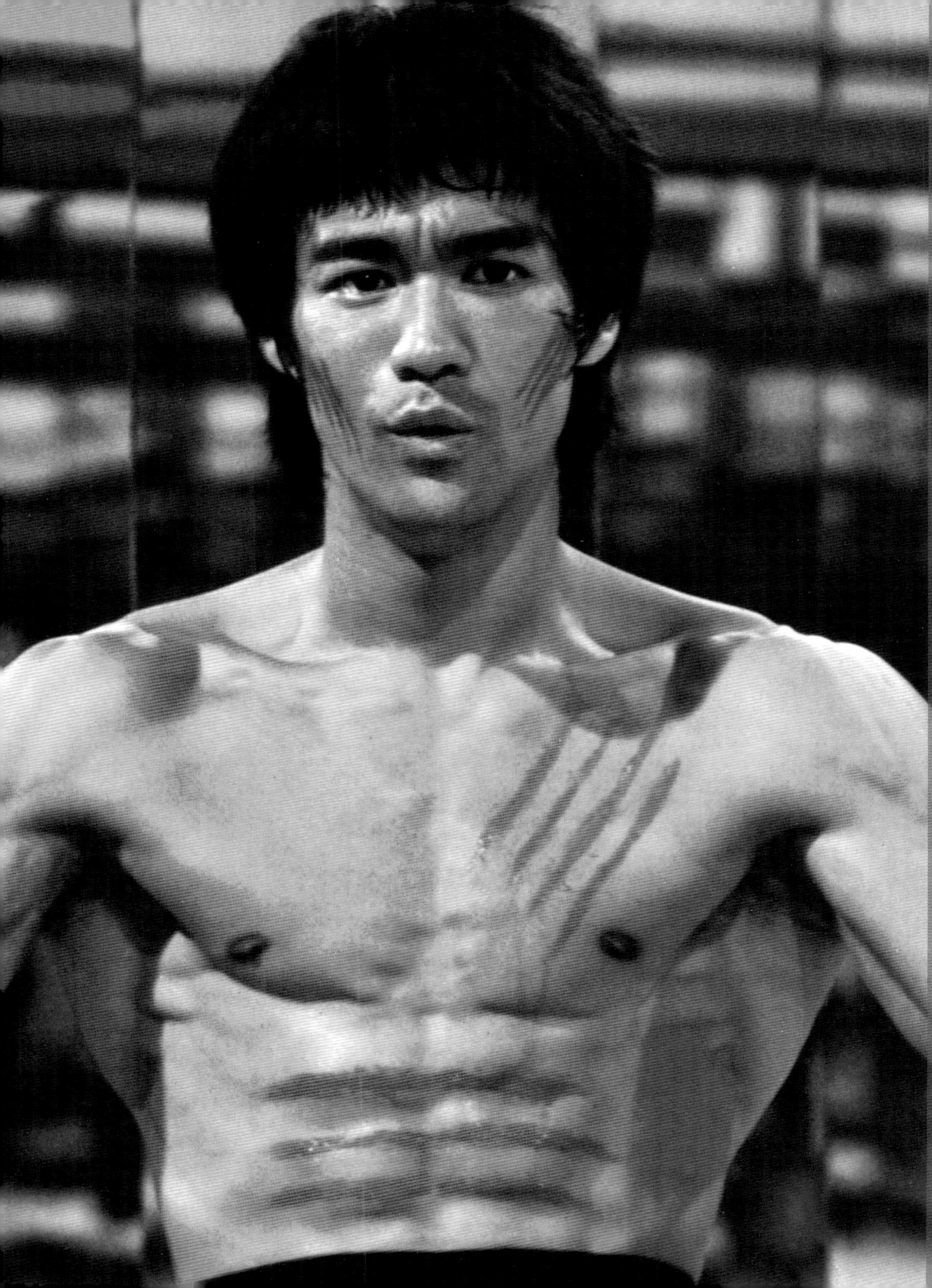

Lee entered Washington University in 1961, combining his regular studies with his ideas for a form of martial arts he called Jeet Kune Do. It incorporated Chinese and Western traditions, and he started teaching fellow students to supplement his income. One of those, Linda Emery, became his wife in 1964. A year later, son Brandon was born, daughter Shannon arriving in 1969.

Having established a martial arts school in Seattle, Lee opened a second at the new family home, Oakland, California. He came to the attention of a producer who was casting for a TV series based on the 1930s radio show *The Green Hornet*. Lee got the part of Kato, sidekick to the crime-busting hero, played by Van Williams. It debuted in late 1966, hoping to match the audience figures of the popular *Batman* series. The production provided the director with an unusual headache, in that Lee's movements were so fast they

were reduced to a blur on screen. He slowed them down, but it didn't save the show, which was cancelled after one season.

Lee picked up the odd acting job – he appeared in the 1969 film *Marlowe*, in which James Garner played Chandler's private eye – and also worked behind the scenes as a fight coordinator. It wasn't enough to sustain him, and he fell back on his teaching, his students including celebrities such as Steve McQueen

'There are no limits. There are only plateaus, and you must not stay there, you must go beyond them.'

featured a Coliseum showdown with Chuck Norris.

Bruce Lee films broke all box-office records in the Asian market, but the star remained determined to crack America. He was in the middle of making *Game of Death* when Hollywood came calling. Warner Brothers had noted his recent successes, which had been dubbed for the Western market, and now wanted to co-produce a blockbuster martial arts movie. *Enter The Dragon (1973)*, in which Lee's character is recruited by the British secret service to break a drug-smuggling ring, became the first Hollywood-backed Kung Fu picture.

After completing filming, Lee returned to Hong Kong to finish *Game of Death*. The project was still running when Lee took a prescription painkiller for a headache. He suffered an allergic reaction that caused a swelling of the brain. He died a week before the premiere of *Enter the Dragon*, aged 32.

Both of Lee's children followed in his footsteps. Brandon made his name in the mid-80s TV sequel *Kung Fu: The Next Generation*. While filming the supernatural thriller *The Crow*, Brandon was killed when a prop gun delivered a lethal charge instead of a blank. He was 28.

Opposite: Bruce Lee and Maria Yi in a scene from the Kung Fu classic Fist of Fury (1972), *filmed in Hong Kong.*

Above: A scene from Enter the Dragon.

Right: Lee pictured with his wife and son Brandon in 1967.

and James Coburn. He sought to break the mould of Chinese actors being portrayed in stereotypical roles by developing his own idea for a TV show. *The Warrior* received a favourable response, eventually aired as *Kung Fu*. Lee was overlooked for the lead role. It was a bitter blow to be told an Asian actor was not bankable; even more galling when David Carradine was made up to give him an Oriental appearance.

The breakthrough in America looked as far away as ever, but *The Green Hornet* had made him a major star in Hong Kong, which became his home once again. His profile was raised several more notches with the release of *The Big Boss* (1971), the first instalment of a three-picture deal with producer Raymond Chow. It had Lee on the trail of a gang of drug smugglers, the poster strapline extolling his physical prowess: 'Every limb of his body is a lethal weapon'. He was on the revenge trail again in *Fist of Fury* (1972), then turned writer-director for his next movie, *Way of the Dragon* (1972), which

Steve McQueen

'KING OF COOL'
24 MARCH 1930 – 7 NOVEMBER 1980

The Magnificent Seven made Steve McQueen an A-list superstar, and he remained one of Hollywood's most bankable actors for two decades. His gift for playing laconic, rebellious characters made him the natural heir to Cagney and Bogart, but with dazzling good looks that also established him as one of the screen's great heart-throbs.

Steve McQueen turned 30 in 1960, the year in which he played Vin in John Sturges's classic western. It had been a long, hard road to the top. He grew up in straitened circumstances in Slater, Missouri, abandoned by his father soon after birth and left to be raised by a feckless mother. He ran wild, often scavenging for food, and petty thieving put him in a Californian reform school at 14. There were desultory manual jobs before his life gained a degree of order with a three-year spell in the Marines, though his anti-authoritarian streak was never tamed. Back on Civvy Street, 21-year-old McQueen landed in New York and fell into acting.

Replacing Ben Gazarra in a 1955 Broadway production of *A Hatful of Rain* gave McQueen's career a major boost. He made his big-screen debut the following year in the boxing biopic *Somebody Up There Likes Me*, playing a bit-part thug in the film that provided Paul Newman with his first headline role. McQueen vowed to be a bigger star than Newman, an unspoken feud that was still rumbling when they co-starred in *The Towering Inferno* 18 years later.

> ' I still have nightmares about being poor, of everything I own just vanishing away. Stardom means that can't happen.'

1958 saw the release of *The Blob*, a piece of science-fiction hokum that became a cult favourite. McQueen's name was finally above the title, and he also starred in the long-running TV western series *Wanted: Dead or Alive*, the show that made him a household name. He was in the middle of his three-year stint as bounty hunter Josh Randall when he landed a meaty role opposite Frank Sinatra in the war drama *Never So Few* (1959). Director John Sturges cast him in *The Magnificent Seven* on the back of that performance

Top: McQueen married actress Neile Adams in 1957. They had two children and were divorced in 1972.

Above: Yul Brynner and McQueen in a scene from The Magnificent Seven *(1960).*

Opposite: McQueen as Lt Frank Bullitt in Peter Yates's thriller.

and he was on his way to becoming the world's top box-office draw.

He was a psychopathic GI in *Hell Is for Heroes* (1962) but it was the glossier, all-star military adventure *The Great Escape* (1963) that brought him his next big hit. McQueen played 'cooler king' Virgil Hilts, whose two-wheeled bid for freedom is one of cinema's most memorable action set pieces. The bike-mad actor came up with the idea and did a lot of his own stunt work, though discretion was called for when it came to the climactic 12-foot jump over a barbed-wire fence.

He was a musician who gets shopgirl Natalie Wood pregnant in *Love with the Proper Stranger* (1963), and a hotshot poker player trying to topple The Man in *The Cincinatti Kid* (1965). Norman Jewison, who directed the latter film and the 1968 caper thriller *The Thomas Crown Affair*, said McQueen was 'the only actor I've

ever taken lines away from who loved it'. He knew that the less he said, the more impact he had. The one time when a pared-down script wasn't acceptable was on *The Towering Inferno* (1974), when McQueen ensured he and Newman had the same number of lines. Then there was the billing battle, the subject of lengthy negotiation. His name appeared top left above the title – Newman's was to the right and slightly higher – which was meant to bestow parity. McQueen was quietly satisfied with the outcome.

By then he had played a maverick cop in the cult crime thriller *Bullitt* (1968), featuring an explosive car chase round the streets of San Francisco, and been on the other side of the law in Sam Peckinpah's *The Getaway* (1972). Co-star Ali McGraw became his second wife, a marriage that soon foundered. *Junior Bonner* (1972), in which he played a fading rodeo star, was a

personal favourite, while he was kicking against the system once again as the eponymous Devil's Island inmate in *Papillon* (1973).

McQueen then left the scene for five years, save for a hirsute appearance in a 1978 screen version of Ibsen's *Enemy of the People*. His final roles saw him back in the saddle in *Tom Horn* (1980) and playing a latter-day Josh Randall in *The Hunter* (1980). Cancer claimed him the year of these films' release.

His 28 films brought one Oscar nomination, for *The Sand Pebbles* (1966). McQueen would not have claimed to be the most versatile or gifted actor, and even though he had studied at the Actors Studio, he was no great technician. But he had charisma and screen presence in spades. That was recognized at the height of his popularity in 1967, when he added his handprint to those cast in cement on Hollywood Walk of Fame. Predictably, McQueen placed his palm the opposite way round to the others.

Above: McQueen dressed to race in Le Mans *(1971).*

Right: Second wife Ali McGraw and McQueen, who is sporting a beard for his role in the movie Papillon. *The pair starred together in* The Getaway.

Opposite: McQueen plays Captain Hilts in John Sturges's classic prisoner-of-war movie The Great Escape.

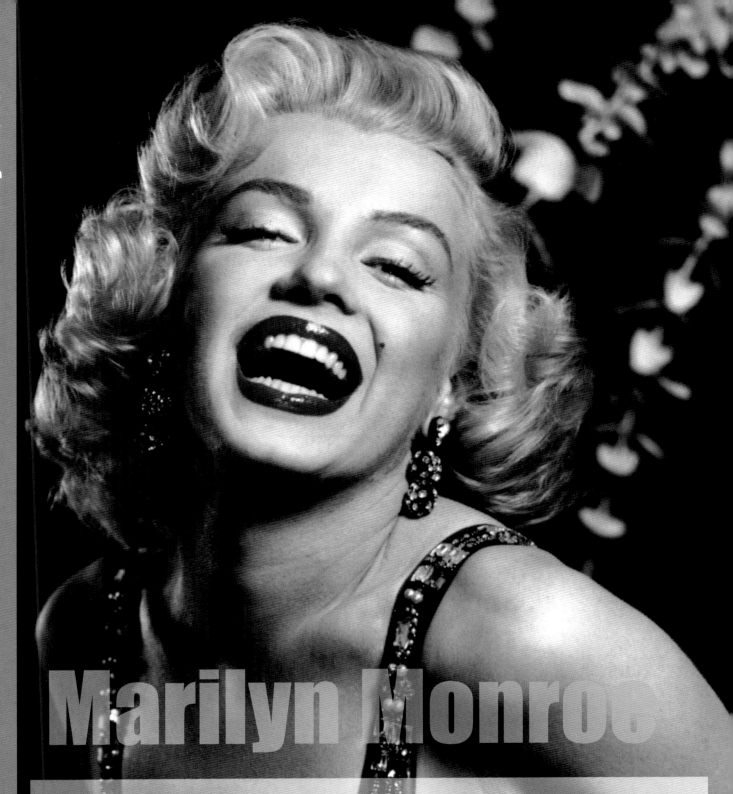

HOLLYWOOD GODDESS
1 JUNE 1926 – 5 AUGUST 1962

The movie industry has had more than its share of rags-to-riches stories, but none has captured the imagination or endured quite like that of Marilyn Monroe. She was the epitome of blonde-bombshell Hollywood glamour, combining sexual allure with childlike vulnerability in a way that gave her a unique appeal.

Norma Jean Baker was born in Los Angeles, yet Tinseltown must have seemed a world away to a young girl bearing the scars of illegitimacy while being bounced around a succession of orphanages and foster homes. Her mother suffered debilitating mental health problems, and Norma Jean's emotional fragility can be traced to childhood years that lacked any semblance of stability or security. Marriage at 16 to James Dougherty wasn't the answer, and even though she picked up some modelling assignments after being spotted while working in an aircraft factory, her career wasn't really taking off. Twentieth Century Fox and Columbia both had her on their books before deciding she was just another dispensable pretty face. Columbia dropped her after *Ladies of the Chorus* (1948), one of the more forgettable offerings from the golden age of screen musicals. By now she had changed her name and dyed her hair; she also posed nude for a calendar that would soon become a collector's item. There was a walk-on part in the Marx Brothers' *Love Happy* (1949), but thereafter the roles were meatier and Monroe proved she had talent to match her physical charms. Her turn as a moll in John Huston's 1950 heist thriller *The Asphalt Jungle* was well received, and Fox re-signed her. This time she had the studio publicity machine behind her, though there were a few unremarkable vehicles before she became a box-office sensation with a trio of releases in 1953, *Niagara, Gentlemen Prefer Blondes* and *How to Marry a Millionaire*. The latter two films revealed a flair for comedy, while her role of gold-digging showgirl Lorelei Lee in *Gentlemen Prefer Blondes* provided the opportunity for a memorably breathy rendition of 'Diamonds Are a Girl's Best Friend'.

Monroe teamed up with Billy Wilder for the first time in *The Seven Year Itch*, playing Tom Ewell's fantasy woman. The scene in which she stands astride a subway grating, skirt billowing, became one of the most famous shots in movie history. It did nothing to assuage Monroe's concerns over the dumb-blonde image that seemed to be her professional lot. Her reaction was to break her contract and head to New York and the

Top: Monroe and Tom Ewell in The Seven Year Itch *(1955), directed by Billy Wilder.*

Right: Marilyn as the bar-room singer Cherie in Joshua Logan's Bus Stop *(1956).*

Opposite: One of a series of images of Marilyn that was later immortalized as a screenprint by Andy Warhol.

famed Actors Studio, where she fell in with a literary set including Arthur Miller. With a short-lived second marriage to baseball legend Joe DiMaggio behind her, Monroe moved from sporting star to cerebral heavyweight for husband number three. She and Miller married in 1956, the year in which her performance as a saloon singer in *Bus Stop* showed that she was more than a mere light comedienne with sex appeal. Monroe needed to be on her mettle to play opposite Laurence Olivier in *The Prince and the Showgirl* (1957).

'I am just a small girl in a big world trying to find someone to love.'

They didn't hit it off – Olivier called her 'a professional amateur' – but the consensus was that she more than held her own in a hit-and-miss production.

Monroe reunited with Wilder to play fragile ukulele player Sugar Kane in the cross-dressing comedy classic *Some Like It Hot* (1959). The director was not alone in being, by turns, entranced and infuriated by his female lead, who was notoriously unreliable on set. Her pill-popping habit was spinning dangerously out of control, such that she needed hospital treatment during the making of *The Misfits* (1961). This, her last completed film, was written by Miller when that marriage, too, was in its death throes. Production of her next planned movie, *Something's Got to Give*, was shut down as her antics tested the studio bosses' patience once too often. The magnetic star had become a liability.

Marilyn Monroe was found dead at her Brentwood home three months later, on the morning of 5 August 1962. She was 36 years old and had starred in just 11 films. There was a history of depression and suicide attempts, and the coroner ruled a self-administered overdose of barbiturates to be the probable cause of death. The fact that she was connected to the very heart of government – involved both with President John F. Kennedy and brother Bobby – fuelled conspiracy theories that persist to this day. Whether any hand but her own played a part in her demise on that August day, it is certainly the case that Monroe was a victim of the system that created her. Joe DiMaggio wanted no Hollywood insiders at her funeral, 'because they had only hurt Marilyn'. Her story is a testament to the American dream, and a salutary tale of the destructive power of fame and success.

Opposite: Joe DiMaggio and Marilyn were married on 14 January 1954 in San Francisco but she filed for divorce less than a year later.

Top: Marilyn poses with Arthur Miller, her third husband, in London. Miller had accompanied his wife to London where she was filming The Prince and the Showgirl *(1957).*

Above: Monroe as Sugar Kane with co-stars Jack Lemmon and Tony Curtis during a break from filming the classic comedy Some Like It Hot *(1959).*

River Phoenix

TEEN IDOL AND ECO-WARRIOR
23 AUGUST 1970 – 31 OCTOBER 1993

In the mid-1980s River Phoenix was lauded as one of Hollywood's brightest new stars. With Adonis looks to match his soaring talent, he was a gift to the celebrity columns until his death from a drug overdose at the age of 23.

River Phoenix had a nomadic, bohemian upbringing. Life experience largely substituted for formal education, and it served him well, as many remarked that he possessed wisdom beyond his years.

He was born River Jude Bottom in Madras, Oregon, the forename taken from the river of life that features in Hermann Hesse's novel *Siddartha*. His parents were drawn to the religious cult The Children of God, which appeared to offer a form of Christianity that fitted with their hippie outlook. Missionary work took them to Venezuela but by the late 1970s they had become disillusioned and returned to the United States. There were now five children, including River's younger sibling Joaquin, another star in the making. All adopted the Phoenix surname as they embarked on a new chapter.

Right: Martha Plimpton and River Phoenix arrive at the 61st Academy Awards ceremony, LA, 1989.

Below: Christine Lahti and River Phoenix in Running on Empty.

Opposite: Phoenix poses, circa 1988.

'**We were constantly moving to different countries and adjusting to new things. It was such a free feeling. I'm glad I didn't have a traditional upbringing.**'

They wound up in LA, where River went on the audition circuit for child actors. He did commercials and TV work before making his feature debut in the teen sci-fi adventure *Explorers* (1985). He followed it up with the coming-of-age drama *Stand by Me* (1986) and The

Mosquito Coast (1986). The latter starred Harrison Ford and the two teamed up again on *Indiana Jones and the Last Crusade* (1989), Phoenix playing the young Indy. For many the pick of his early films was *Running on Empty (1988)*, for which he was Oscar-nominated.

Phoenix used his star status to promote veganism, the ethical treatment of animals and his environmentalist agenda. He also devoted time to music, performing in the band Aleka's Attic, which attracted the interest of Island Records. One of his final screen outings, *The Thing Called Love* (1993),

revolved around aspiring musicians trying to make it in Nashville. But many consider Phoenix's turn as a hustler in *My Own Private Idaho* (1991) as the high point of a brief, dazzling career.

River Phoenix was in the middle of a troubled shoot when, on the night of 30 October 1993, he spent the evening at LA's Viper Room nightspot. It was after midnight when he staggered out onto the street and collapsed, the autopsy report revealing the actor with a clean-living reputation had a cocktail of drugs in his system. The film he was making, a thriller called *Dark Blood*, remained uncompleted.

Christopher Reeve

CINEMA'S MAN OF STEEL
25 SEPTEMBER 1952 – 10 OCTOBER 2004

Christopher Reeve shot to stardom playing an invincible comic-book hero. Paralysed from the neck down in a riding accident, he inspired others with his indomitable spirit, continuing to act while campaigning for research into spinal-cord injuries.

Christopher Reeve was a New Yorker by birth, the son of writer-academic Franklin Reeve and journalist Barbara Johnson. He developed a love of theatre while studying at Princeton Day School and Cornell University, and showed he had talent to match his ambition by being accepted into the prestigious Juilliard School of Performing Arts.

Early acting credits included Enid Bagnold's *A Matter of Gravity*, in which he shared a Broadway stage with Katharine Hepburn. There was also a stint in the long-running TV soap *Love of Life*. Reeve broke into film with a bit-part in the submarine disaster flick *Gray Lady Down* (1978), and was largely unknown when he landed the role of Superman in that year's blockbuster production. His chiselled good looks and granite-hewn 6 ft 4 inch-frame made him a perfect choice for a role to which he returned three times over the next decade.

Concerned about typecasting, he signed up to a diverse range of projects including the romantic drama *Somewhere in Time* (1980), Ira Levin's thriller *Deathtrap* (1982) and the Merchant-Ivory period pieces *The Bostonians* (1984) and *The Remains of the Day* (1993).

> ' A hero is an ordinary individual who finds the strength to persevere and endure in spite of overwhelming obstacles.'

Reeve juggled film and stage work, the latter including the role of a paraplegic Vietnam veteran in *Fifth of July*, which opened on Broadway in 1980. Fifteen years after starring in that production, Reeve, a passionate and accomplished horseman, had the riding accident that damaged his spinal cord. He overcame depression and vowed to walk again, but the victories, when they came, were small. He did regain some movement and feeling, and was eventually able to breathe without the aid of a ventilator for long periods.

He returned to work playing a wheelchair-bound voyeur in a 1998 remake of Hitchcock's *Rear Window*, picking up a Screen Actors Guild award for the role made famous by James Stewart. Initially apprehensive about taking up the challenge, he said: 'I was surprised to find that if I really concentrated, and just let the thoughts happen, that they would read on my face.' But the main preoccupation of his later years was lobbying for more research into spinal injuries. Five years after his death, President Barack Obama enacted the Christopher and Dana Reeve Paralysis Act, whose aim was to improve the quality of life of sufferers while pushing back the scientific boundaries.

Left: Reeve with his wife Dana in 1989.

Above: Photographed with close friend and Juilliard classmate Robin Williams in 1979.

Opposite: Reeve as Superman, the role that catapulted him into the Hollywood A list in 1978.

149

John Ritter

'GOOFY EVERYMAN'
17 SEPTEMBER 1948 – 11 SEPTEMBER 2003

John Ritter made his name as lovable, accident-prone chef Jack Tripper in the 1970s hit TV series *Three's Company*. A marvellous physical comedian, he was given the 'goofy Everyman' tag by his second wife, Amy Yasbeck.

Show business was in John Ritter's blood. Father Tex appeared in countless westerns and was a singing star and his mother Dorothy Fay was also an established actress who became the official 'greeter' at Nashville's *Grand Ole Opry*. John made his big-screen debut in 1971 in Disney's *The Barefoot Executive*. He appeared in the period comedy *Nickelodeon* (1976), the biblical spoof *Wholly Moses!* (1980) and even turned up in a

spooky horror flick *The Other* (1972). But it was TV that made him a star. Ritter guested on numerous top-rated shows, including *MASH* and *Kojak*, and had a regular slot on *The Waltons* as Reverend Matthew Fordwick.

Below: With Three's Company *co-stars Joyce DeWitt and Suzanne Somers, 1978.*

Opposite: John Ritter pictured at the time of the launch of 8 Simple Rules for Dating My Teenage Daughter.

'If I found a cure for a huge disease, while I was hobbling up onstage to accept the Nobel Prize they'd be playing the theme song from "Three's Company".'

The red-letter year was 1977, when *Three's Company* first aired. The set-up of three singletons sharing an apartment proved to be a ratings winner. Ritter received a Golden Globe and an Emmy for his portrayal of Jack Tripper, the sole male in the group, pretending to be gay to appease a prudish landlord. No sooner had the show ended its seven-year run than Ritter carried the same character over into the spin-off *Three's a Crowd*. He scored well with other TV comedy dramas such as *Hooperman*, made by his own production company, and continued his big-screen career with films including *Real Men* (1987) and *Skin Deep* (1989).

Spots on shows such as *Ally McBeal* and *Buffy the Vampire Slayer* helped Ritter maintain his enormous popularity among audiences. He also picked up a Theater World award for his performance in Neil Simon's *The Dinner Party*, which opened on Broadway in 2000. But it was another TV sitcom that was the high point of his late career: *8 Simple Rules for Dating My Teenage Daughter*, which launched in 2002, saw Ritter playing a columnist handing out advice while struggling with his own parental responsibilities. The 54-year-old actor collapsed on set while working on the show and died later in hospital. He was treated for a heart attack, but the cause of death was subsequently confirmed as an aortic dissection, a congenital heart defect. Ritter's last movie, *Bad Santa* (2003), was dedicated to his memory.

Romy Schneider

TRAGIC ACTRESS
23 SEPTEMBER 1938 – 29 MAY 1982

Romy Schneider emerged as one of German cinema's leading actresses in the 1950s and went on to become an international screen star. Her private life was touched by tragedy, and she died, grief-stricken, aged 43.

Born Rosemarie Albach-Retty in Vienna, Schneider's father Wolf was a well-known stage and screen actor, while her mother Magda Schneider was a popular star of Austrian and German films. Magda smoothed her teenage daughter's path into the performing arts, playing her screen mother in several films in the 1950s. Three of those saw Romy cast as Elizabeth, a 19th-century Bavarian empress. Collectively known as the 'Sissi' series, these historical romps were enormously popular, though Schneider tried hard to shake off a sugary character that stuck to her 'like oatmeal'.

She enticed heart-throb actor Alain Delon in *Christine* (1958), a passion that continued off set. Their five-year affair ended when Schneider learned in a scribbled note that Delon had left her for another woman. They later renewed their friendship and worked together on *The Swimming Pool* (1969) and Joseph Losey's *The Assassination of Trotsky* (1972).

Schneider reached an international audience with *Boccaccio '70* (1962), a portmanteau production including a Visconti-directed piece in which she played a wife stirred to action when she discovers her husband's sexual peccadilloes. That same year she appeared in Orson Welles's adaptation of Kafka's bureaucratic nightmare *The Trial*. Hollywood beckoned, and Schneider joined Jack Lemmon for the knockabout comedy *Good Neighbour Sam* (1964), and was part of the all-star cast of *What's New Pussycat?* (1965).

'I have the feeling that I was born in Vienna in order to live in Paris.'

She made most of her late-career films in France, where she lived for many years and was greatly esteemed. When that country introduced its own awards – the Césars – in 1975, Schneider took the inaugural Best Actress laurels for *L'important c'est d'aimer* and starred in the *Le Vieux Fusil*. which was named Best Film. She scooped the top acting prize again in 1979 for *Une Histoire Simple*.

Schneider's first husband, stage director Harry Meyen, committed suicide, and their 14-year-old son was killed in 1981 when he was impaled on spikes while climbing a fence. Her second marriage ended the same year. Schneider never recovered from these bitter personal blows. The following year, she was found dead in her Paris apartment, alcohol and pills said to have contributed to her fatal heart attack.

An award for aspiring actresses working in the French film industry was instituted in her honour in 1984. Winners of the Prix Romy Schneider include Juliette Binoche and Vanessa Paradis.

Top: Schneider with French actor Alain Delon shortly after they announced their engagement in 1959.

Above: Schneider in the role of Sissi, circa 1955.

Opposite: A portrait dating from the early 1970s.

CULT LEADER'S STAR VICTIM
25 JANUARY 1943 – 9 AUGUST 1969

Sharon Tate was a rising Hollywood star when she was brutally murdered in her home by followers of cult leader Charles Manson. He knew the property's previous celebrity occupants and wanted the attack to foment a race war. For Sharon it was a case of wrong place, wrong time.

Sharon Tate won the first of many beauty contests before her first birthday. Her looks, charm and grace would be her passport into the acting world, initially as an extra in films shot on location in Italy, where her army officer father was posted in the early 1960s.

Commercials and modelling assignments followed, though it was unclear whether she had any acting talent. Even so, Filmways thought she had potential and signed her to a seven-year deal. As part of the grooming process, Tate appeared in the popular TV

Tate and Polanski married in England in January 1968, the beautiful ingénue and fêted auteur becoming a golden celebrity couple. By then she had added the beach farce *Don't Make Waves* (1967) and an adaptation of Jacqueline Susann's *Valley of the Dolls* (1967) to her résumé. Her frustration over the parts she was being offered dissipated when she found she was pregnant early in 1969. A Los Angeles family home was needed, and Tate just had time to unpack at 10050 Cielo Drive before departing for France to make the comedy *The 13 Chairs*. She returned in July; Polanski had business in London.

On 9 August Sharon, Jay Sebring and two houseguests dined together. All four bodies were discovered the following morning. In March 1971 cult leader Charles Manson and four acolytes were convicted of those murders and three others that had been carried out in a random two-day killing spree.

'My whole life has been decided by fate. I've never planned anything that's happened to me.'

comedy show *The Beverly Hillbillies*, sporting a dark wig to avoid too much attention. By 1967 Filmways decided it was time to launch her movie career, and she travelled to Europe to play, fittingly, a bewitching young girl in the occult thriller *Eye of the Devil*. Director J. Lee Thompson said she had 'star projection'.

More horror followed in the shape of *The Fearless Vampire Killers* (1967), this time with tongue firmly in cheek. Romance blossomed between Sharon and the film's writer-director Roman Polanski, the actress cutting her ties with former love, celebrity hair stylist Jay Sebring. It was an amicable parting, Sebring remaining a close friend.

Above: Sharon Tate and co-stars in a publicity still for Valley of the Dolls.

Top left: Tate in The Fearless Vampire Killers.

Opposite: Roman Polanski and Sharon Tate on their wedding day, 20 January 1968, London.

Rudolph Valentino

THE GREAT LATIN LOVER
6 MAY 1895 – 23 AUGUST 1926

Valentino's smouldering sensuousness and exotic appeal had a swoon-inducing effect on women. There was mass hysteria – some fans reportedly driven to suicide – when his lifeless body was put on public view in New York.

Rodolpho di Valentina d'Antonguolla was born in the southern Italian city of Castellaneta. He made an unpromising start to his adult life, first in the military, then as an agriculture student. He arrived in New York aged 18, seeking a fresh start. Had it not been for his dancing talent, Valentino may have been stuck in menial jobs, perhaps even a life of crime, for he soon became known to the city's police force. His lightness of foot brought him stage work, and at a friend's suggestion he decided to try his luck in Hollywood.

Ironically, his exotic looks initially counted against him. Early bit-part screen outings saw him playing louche characters, or trading on his dancing skills. He was given leading man status in *A Society Sensation* (1918), but a year later was reduced to the role of Apache dancer in *A Rogue's Romance*. Producers didn't see him as star material. The likes of Mae Murray – whom he befriended in New York – pleaded his cause, and he cavorted with both sexes to help advance his career. Yet he seemed destined to be shunted round the studios as a minor player.

That changed in 1921 with *The Four Horsemen of the Apocalypse*, in which he played shiftless Argentine Julio, who becomes a war hero. He also dances a seductive tango in a bar-room scene, which sparked a craze and made him an overnight sensation. Director Rex Ingram expanded his part when he saw the early rushes, and Valentino's name was hastily pushed up the billing.

> **'Women are not in love with me but with the picture of me on the screen. I am merely the canvas on which women paint their dreams.'**

Left: Valentino and actress Natacha Rambova sign the register on their wedding day, 14 March 1923.

Opposite: Rudolph Valentino in the desert adventure, The Son of the Sheik.

The film made Metro over $4 million, which Valentino felt qualified him for a hefty salary increase. The studio blanched, and he signed to Paramount, who reaped the box-office benefits of *The Sheik* (1921) and *Blood and Sand* (1922). He tried to exert more creative control with *The Young Rajah* (1922), which was roundly panned, though revealing costumes kept enough fans happy. He had just made *The Son of the Sheik* (1926) when he died from an infection following surgery on a perforated ulcer. Valentino may not have been a great actor but he was a screen legend.

Natalie Wood

LUMINOUS SCREEN BEAUTY
20 JULY 1938 – 29 NOVEMBER 1981

Groomed for stardom by a pushy stage mother, Natalie Wood was a child performer who blossomed into an Oscar-nominated actress.

Natalie Wood's parents were Russian émigrés who came to America separately in the 1930s. Nikolai and Maria Zakharenko adopted the name Gurdin after their marriage in 1938, the year Natalia was born in San Francisco. Maria was a movie-mad fantasist who heeded a fortune teller's prediction that her second daughter would be a famous beauty. From the

moment of Natalia's birth her mother lavished all her attention upon her and told her she was destined for great things.

By 1943 the family were living in Santa Rosa, California, and when a film crew arrived to make *Happy Land*, Maria ensured her four-year-old was noticed. She was billed as Natalie Wood for her next screen outing, *Tomorrow Is Forever* (1946). Already she was feeling the weight of expectation exerted by her single-minded mother. At a screen test requiring tears, Maria 'prepared' her by pulling the wings off a butterfly.

Natalie appeared in the perennial Christmas favourite *Miracle on 34th Street* and *The Ghost And Mrs Muir* (both 1947). She almost drowned while making *The Green Promise* (1949), an event that left her with a water phobia.

> # 'I spent practically all my time in the company of adults. I was very withdrawn, very shy, I did what I was told and I tried not to disappoint anybody.'

Her role as James Dean's sweetheart in *Rebel Without a Cause* (1955) brought a Supporting Actress Oscar nomination, and she was short-listed in the main category for *Splendour in the Grass* (1961). That year also saw the release of *West Side Story*, in which she played the star-crossed Juliet figure. Her singing voice was dubbed, but the performance was memorable.

In 1962 her five-year marriage to Robert Wagner ended. They would remarry a decade later, but during their time apart, Wood married British producer Richard Gregson, the union producing daughter Natasha.

Wood's portrayal of a pregnant shopgirl in *Love with the Proper Stranger* (1963) brought further Academy recognition. Other starring roles include *Gypsy* (1962), *Inside Daisy Clover* (1966) and the sex comedy *Bob & Carol & Ted & Alice* (1969). Her remarriage to Wagner produced a second daughter, and film appearances became sporadic. She returned to the screen in 1979 with the disaster movie *Meteor*, and won a Golden Globe for the TV miniseries *From Here to Eternity*, in the role made famous by Deborah Kerr.

Her final film was the sci-fi feature *Brainstorm*. On Thanksgiving weekend 1981, Wood and Wagner were sailing off Catalina Island on their yacht *Splendour*. Her *Brainstorm* co-star Christopher Walken joined the party, during which the 43-year-old actress drowned under mysterious circumstances.

Top: Wood pictured with husband Robert Wagner, second time around.

Above: James Dean and Natalie in Rebel Without a Cause.

Opposite: A publicity picture taken in 1961.

Sports Stars

Arthur Ashe

TENNIS TRAILBLAZER
10 JULY 1943 – 6 FEBRUARY 1993

Arthur Ashe overcame considerable prejudice on his way to becoming the first African American to make it to the top in men's tennis. Throughout his career Ashe used his position to help others, and his final months were spent raising awareness about AIDS.

Arthur Ashe's early years in Richmond, Virginia, were not easy. He lost his mother when he was six, and took up a sport where segregation and discrimination were rife. Ashe first wielded a racket on the local recreation ground, which his father policed for a living. His game improved under the watchful eye of Robert Walter Johnson, a physician who made it his mission to give talented black youngsters a helping hand in an era when so many doors were slammed shut. Multiple grand-slam winner Althea Gibson was one whose career he promoted; Ashe would be his next big success.

'From what we get we can make a living; what we give, however, makes a life.'

He graduated from UCLA in 1966, by which time he had already represented the USA in the Davis Cup. In 1968, the start of the Open era, Ashe claimed his first major title, beating Tom Okker in the US Open final on the grass of Forest Hills. Later that year he helped the US wrest the Davis Cup back from Australia. Ashe had to get used to seeing the words *first black player to* in reports of his successes, and they were trotted out again after his victories in the 1970 Australian Open – by which time he had joined the professional ranks – and at Wimbledon five years later. In the latter final he

beat holder and top seed Jimmy Connors, who hadn't dropped a set in the tournament and was hot favourite to retain his title. Ashe was imperturbable on court, a flamboyant shotmaker with impeccable demeanour.

Criticism came his way when he played in South Africa in 1973, some members of the black community unhappy over his decision to compete in a country riven by apartheid. The mild-mannered, forthright Ashe thought the integration cause was best served by his presence. His erudition also made him a natural choice for the role of ATP president.

Heart-bypass surgery in 1979 precipitated the end of his playing days, but he went on to captain a Davis Cup-winning team, and worked tirelessly to give inner-city kids the chance to play the sport he graced for two decades.

In 1988 Ashe discovered he had AIDS, the infection probably dating from a second heart operation five years earlier. 1988 also saw the publication of his three-volume opus *A Hard Road to Glory*, in which he chronicled the achievements of black American athletes. Ashe's own accomplishments on and off the court make him one of tennis's finest ambassadors as well as a great champion.

Opposite: Ashe plays a backhand at Wimbledon, 1975.

Below: Arthur Ashe pictured with fellow American Jimmy Connors, 1975.

Seve Ballesteros

GOLF COURSE CONJUROR
9 APRIL 1957 – 7 MAY 2011

Seve Ballesteros was golf's teenage glamour boy, a player who attracted legions of new fans with his swashbuckling style. He was Europe's 'Arnold Palmer and Jack Nicklaus rolled into one', according to his Ryder Cup captain Bernard Gallacher.

Sports fans enjoy poring over statistics, and Seve Ballesteros's make for impressive reading: 87 titles, including 5 majors; 6 European Order of Merit successes; 5 World Match Play wins; 5 Ryder Cup victories as player and captain. And yet in Ballesteros's case they fail to tell the whole story, for it was the style as much as the substance for which he is remembered: the élan, the verve, the sheer audacity he displayed; the ability to conjure up miraculous recovery shots when all hope seemed lost.

'It doesn't matter where you hit the drive if you make the putt.'

He grew up in Pedreña, a village on the northern coast of Spain. The family income came from farming, but there was also considerable sporting talent in the blood, including a golf-pro uncle. Seve became a caddie at his local club, developing his skills on the beaches until he was officially allowed to use the facilities. That honour was granted at the age of 12, after he won the caddies' championship.

Below: Seve strikes the ball at the World Match Play Championship at Wentworth in 1976.

Left: José María Olazábal and Seve share an anxious moment at the Ryder Cup, Muirfield Village, Ohio, 1987.

Opposite: Seve displays the claret jug at Royal Lytham & St Annes, July 1988.

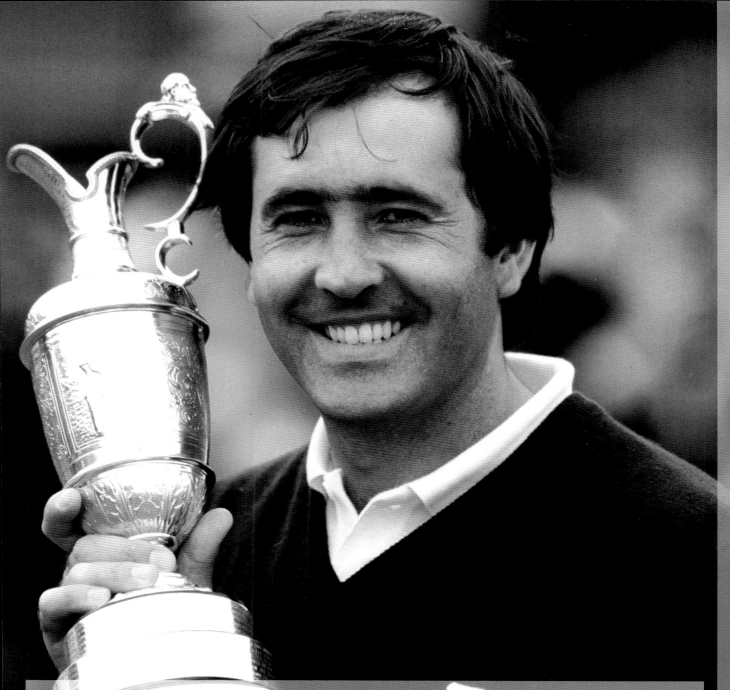

Seve turned professional in 1974, but it was two years later, when he finished runner-up to Johnny Miller at Royal Birkdale, that he drew the world's attention. Three years later he went one better, claiming his first Open championship at Royal Lytham. The wayward drives and jaw-dropping recovery shots were much in evidence that week, including one birdie secured despite a car-park detour.

In 1980 Ballesteros became Masters champion – at 23 the youngest player to win at Augusta until Tiger Woods lowered the bar – and was fitted for a second green jacket three years later. The 1984 and 1988 Open titles rounded out his successes in the majors.

Ballesteros competed in eight Ryder Cups between 1979 and 1995, forming a record-breaking partnership with compatriot José María Olazábal. He was a talismanic figure, helping Europe to a maiden victory in 1985 and a first win on US soil two years later. Home success at the Belfry in 1989 brought up a hat-trick, and Seve was part of the team that regained the spoils at Oak Hill in 1995. He captained the side to victory at Valderrama in 1997.

Ballesteros retired in 2007, having been dogged by back problems. A year later, a brain tumour was discovered, the start of a three-year battle he was eventually to lose.

Roberto Clemente

'EXAMPLE AND GLORY OF PUERTO RICO'
18 AUGUST 1934 – 31 DECEMBER 1972

As a star outfielder for the Pittsburgh Pirates, Roberto Clemente became a national hero in his native Puerto Rico. His status was further enhanced when he died on a mercy mission trying to help earthquake victims.

Roberto Clemente was a baseball fanatic as a child, developing his bullet throwing arm as he practised in the fields around his home town of Carolina. He played in the amateur league in his mid-teens, and was then recruited to the pro ranks with Santurce Crabbers. After a brief spell with Brooklyn Dodgers' minor league subsidiary, he joined Pittsburgh Pirates in the 1954 draft.

It took him a while to adjust, but by the end of the decade Clemente was a dominant force in the game. Of that famous rifle arm, one commentator once said, 'he could field the ball in New York and throw out a guy in Pennsylvania'. At bat he was equally effective, topping the National League four times, hitting a career average .317 and scoring 240 home runs and joining an elite group who had reached the magical figure of 3,000 hits.

In 1960 Pittsburgh won the championship pennant and beat the Yankees in the World Series, Clemente shining in both. The following year he won the first of 12 Gold Gloves for his performances in the field. He led the league in hits in 1964 and 1967, and was named Most Valuable Player (MVP) of 1966.

'I want to be remembered as a ballplayer who gave all he had to give.'

In 1971 Clemente starred in the Pirates' World Series win over hot favourites Baltimore Orioles, Clemente hitting a home run in the decisive game and being named MVP of the series.

Even as a fêted, highly paid sporting star, Clemente never lost the common touch. He once said: 'Any time you have an opportunity to make a difference in this world and you don't, then you are wasting your time on Earth.' He showed those weren't empty words when Nicaragua was struck by a devastating earthquake in December 1972. Clemente helped organize relief flights, and as rumours circulated that aid was being diverted, he decided to go in person. The heavily laden plane went down in the sea shortly after taking off from San Juan on New Year's Eve. Clemente's body was never recovered.

Baseball honoured one of its greatest players by inducting Roberto Clemente into the Hall of Fame, waiving the usual five-year post-career wait. A statue outside the Roberto Clemente Stadium in his native land bears the inscription: 'Example And Glory Of Puerto Rico'.

Top: Clemente slides back into first base as Boog Powell waits on the throw, October 1971.

Opposite: Clemente in the on-deck circle, waiting his turn to bat at Three Rivers Stadium in Pittsburgh, Pennsylvania.

Above: Clemente bats against the Baltimore Orioles during Game 1 of the 1971 World Series.

Maureen Connolly

'LITTLE MO'
17 SEPTEMBER 1934 – 21 JUNE 1969

In the brief period she enjoyed at the top before a freak injury ended her career, tennis prodigy Maureen Connolly swept all before her, the first woman to win the calendar grand slam.

armoury the fearsome groundstrokes that would bring her 9 grand slam singles titles from the 11 championships she contested. Her serve and volleying were initially moderate in comparison, but those raking drives, allied to her remarkable focus and

> ## 'All I ever see is my opponent. You could set off dynamite in the next court and I wouldn't notice.'

Maureen Connolly was a powerhouse player in a diminutive 5 ft 3 inch frame. Her remorseless baseline hitting wore down bigger and more experienced opponents, earning her the 'Little Mo' soubriquet – the pocket-sized version of the battleship *Missouri*.

She grew up in San Diego, taking her first steps in the game at her local club under the tutelage of resident pro Wilbur Folsom. It was he who advised her to switch to playing right-handed, Mo having started out as a leftie. By the age of 14 she already had in her

Above: Mo accompanied by her coach Eleanor Tennant.

Left: Keeping her eye on the ball in 1953.

Opposite: Mo stands by the net in 1953.

sheer will to win, were the key to her success. She practised indefatigably, usually against quality male opponents to give her the edge in competition.

Connolly's game progressed under the guidance of celebrated coach Eleanor 'Teach' Tennant, guru to many Hollywood stars as well as tennis professionals of both sexes. Tennant was a stern taskmaster who steered Mo to victory in the 1951 US Championships. At 16 she became the youngest-ever winner of the title, beating compatriot Shirley Fry in the final.

In 1952 Connolly and Tennant clashed at Wimbledon, the coach wanting her to withdraw as she was nursing a shoulder injury. Mo fired her and went on to win the first in a hat-trick of Wimbledon titles. Louise Brough was her victim this time. This Wimbledon success was the start of a run of six consecutive wins in the majors. However, 1953 was Connolly's *annus mirabilis*, when she won a clean sweep of the slams, a feat that only Margaret Court and Steffi Graf have since equalled.

Just before the 1954 US Championships, 19-year-old Connolly was indulging her other great passion, horse-riding, when an accident involving a truck left her with leg injuries that ended her career. She maintained her interest in the sport through coaching and media work, and raised a family with her husband, an Olympic-standard equestrian. 'Little Mo' Connolly lost a three-year battle with cancer on the eve of the 1969 Wimbledon championships. She was 34.

'THE INTIMIDATOR'
29 APRIL 1951 – 18 FEBRUARY 2001

Dale Earnhardt was a dominant force in NASCAR for two decades, champion driver on seven occasions. He had over 70 race victories to his name when he died while competing in the 2001 Daytona 500, the most prestigious event in the NASCAR calendar.

The man whose uncompromising style earned him the 'Intimidator' nickname and the respect of his peers grew up in Kannapolis, North Carolina. Father Ralph was himself no mean driver, and Dale

couldn't get out of school quickly enough to follow in his wheeltracks. He began his illustrious 27-year career in top-level competition in 1975, but his breakthrough season came four years later when

'Finishing races is important, but racing is more important.'

he took the first of his 76 victories, finishing 7th overall and taking the Rookie of the Year award. Twelve months later he bagged the first of his Winston Cup titles. No other driver had won the sport's top honour so soon after picking up the rookie laurels.

A frustrating few seasons followed that triumph, Earnhardt at one point dropping out of the top ten – something that happened just twice between 1979 and 2000, his last full season of competition. But 1986 brought a second championship and began a remarkable run in which he lifted the title six times in nine years. 1987 was his most dominant campaign, Earnhardt racking up 11 victories in 29 races. One of those came in the Winston, a race run at Charlotte Motor Speedway, where he doggedly fought off the challenge of rival Bill Elliott. At one point he careered onto the infield turf, but retained control and held on to first place as he rejoined the track. The 'pass in the grass' has become part of NASCAR folklore, a prime example of the fearless daring that was Earnhardt's hallmark.

By the mid-1990s, he had equalled Richard Petty's record of seven championships. The glaring omission from his résumé was victory in the blue riband event, the Daytona 500. Earnhardt ended that 20-year quest in 1998, taking the chequered flag with an average speed of 172.712 mph. Still good enough to take the runner-up spot in the 2000 championship, Earnhardt was killed the following year while attempting to capture his second Daytona 500. His son, Dale Jr, was contesting the lead in the final stages when Earnhardt, in the thick of the chasing pack, was involved in a fatal collision.

Opposite: Earnhardt pictured in 1985 when he drove the Wrangler Jeans Chevrolet for Richard Childress Racing.

Below: Dale Earnhardt Sr poses with his son at the raceway in Daytona Beach, Florida, 2001.

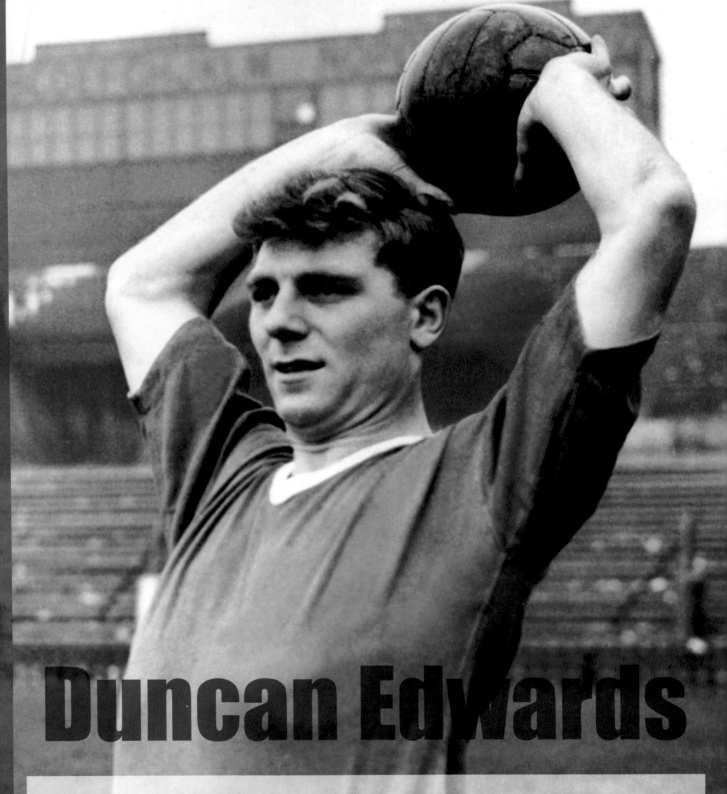

Duncan Edwards

ONE-MAN TEAM
1 OCTOBER 1936 – 21 FEBRUARY 1958

Manchester United's dazzling young 1950s team looked set to dominate English and European football when it was ripped apart on a slush-piled Munich runway. Duncan Edwards was a diamond in a side packed with gems.

Precious little footage exists of Duncan Edwards in action, hence any appraisal – statistics apart – rests largely on the testimony of his contemporaries: teammates, opponents, bosses and fans. The consistency of view is astonishing. By all accounts he was, if not quite a one-man team, certainly one who could play anywhere and shine. 'Big Dunc' had no weakness; silky skills in a battering-ram frame, equally effective in the heart of the defence or rampaging upfield. Teammate Bobby Charlton, a legend in his own right, said that Edwards was the only player who made him feel inferior.

He grew up in Dudley, a town in England's industrial heartlands. Apart from football, folk dancing was the main interest of the young schoolboy. Edwards moved through the representative ranks at a dizzying speed, helped by the fact that he had a superb physique. Just shy of 5 ft 11 inches fully grown, his barrel chest and tree-trunk legs made him appear of more mountainous stature.

The race for his signature was won by Manchester United, for whom he made his first-team debut aged 16 in April 1953. He was soon a fixture in the side, a pivotal player in the team that won back-to-back championships in 1956 and 1957. These young lions were dubbed the 'Busby Babes' after their astute, inspirational manager. Matt Busby assembled an all-conquering team, and he, too, singled out Edwards as 'the player who had everything'.

Edwards was an England international by the age of 18. He looked set to add to an already impressive list of credits for club and country when he was killed in the Munich air disaster, which claimed the lives of seven other players and ended the career of others. After a refuelling stop in Munich, the BEA plane crashed on its third attempt to get airborne. Edwards suffered appalling injuries, including a collapsed lung, damaged kidneys and multiple fractures. He died 15 days later.

'Get stuck in!'

In one of his last bouts of consciousness, Edwards enquired of United's assistant manager what time the next game kicked off. Told it was three o'clock on Saturday, as usual, 21-year-old Edwards uttered his final words: 'Get stuck in!'

Above: Duncan Edwards training in January 1954 after being selected for England's Under 23 team at the age of just 17.

Opposite: Edwards takes a throw-in, April 1957.

173

Lou Gehrig

'THE IRON HORSE'
19 JUNE 1903 – 2 JUNE 1941

Baseball legend Lou Gehrig set numerous records in a glory-filled career with the New York Yankees. He also gave his name to the degenerative disease that claimed his life at 37.

The son of German immigrants, Lou Gehrig was born and raised in the city where he became a sporting superstar. He went to Columbia University on a football scholarship in 1921, but by the end of his second year, Gehrig's baseball skills had attracted the attention of a Yankees scout. By 1925 Gehrig was a fixture in the team, clocking up 2,130 consecutive appearances over the next 14 years. X-rays revealed that he sustained a number of fractures during that time, showing that the 'Iron Horse' nickname was well merited.

In 1926 Gehrig topped the all-important .300 mark for his batting, a feat he would match in each of the next dozen seasons. A career average of .340, with 493 home runs and 1,995 runs batted in (RBI) to his name, puts him in the top echelon of baseball stars. Of the many stand-out campaigns, 1927 has gone down as one of the great individual and team performances, Gehrig hitting 47 home runs, second only to his illustrious teammate Babe Ruth. The Yankees trounced the Pittsburgh Pirates in the World Series, and Gehrig took the first of his

> **'I consider myself the luckiest man on the face of the earth.'**

Above: Lou Gehrig poses with fellow legend Babe Ruth, 1939.

Left: Gehrig at Yankee Stadium before a game in 1925.

Opposite: A watchful Gehrig stands in the field, circa 1935.

Most Valuable Player (MVP) awards. He would play a pivotal role in six victorious World Series campaigns.

As time caught up on Ruth – who was eight years his senior – Gehrig came into his own. In June 1932 he hit four home runs in a single game, and two years later took the Triple Crown with a .363 batting average, 49 home runs and 165 RBIs. Following Ruth's departure after the 1934 season, he starred alongside Joe DiMaggio in an unstoppable Yankees side.

Gehrig's unbroken run ended when his form dipped and he took himself off the team in May 1939. Within weeks he was diagnosed as suffering from the degenerative disease amyotrophic lateral sclerosis. A special tribute was laid on at the Yankee Stadium on 4 July, when Gehrig spoke movingly about the good fortune that tempered the 'bad break' he'd been given. He was fast-tracked into baseball's Hall of Fame and his famous No 4 jersey was retired. A year after his death, Lou Gehrig's story was told in the biopic *Pride of the Yankees*, Gary Cooper playing an all-American hero loved for his humility as well as his sporting prowess.

Bruce McLaren

F1 RACER AND TEAM FOUNDER
30 AUGUST 1937 – 2 JUNE 1970

Bruce McLaren was in the vanguard of an Antipodean assault on the Formula One championship in the late 1950s. He became the youngest-ever race winner and founded the team that has lifted the title on a dozen occasions.

'To do something well is so worthwhile that to die trying to do it better cannot be foolhardy.'

Auckland-born Bruce McLaren came from racing stock, his garage-owner father competing on two wheels. In childhood he had to overcome Perthes disease, a degenerative hip-joint condition that put him in traction for a lengthy period and left him with a limp. He began his competitive career in hill climbing, moving on to circuit racing while also studying engineering.

Having made a name for himself in his native land, 20-year-old McLaren was granted a scholarship that took him to Europe. He took the step up in class in his stride and he was snapped up by Cooper to compete in the elite division in 1959.

His Aussie teammate Jack Brabham took the title that year, but McLaren claimed his first win, at the inaugural US Grand Prix staged at Sebring. At 22 years 104 days, he was the youngest race winner in the championship's history, a record that stood until Fernando Alonso's victory in Hungary in 2003.

That maiden success helped McLaren to a highly respectable sixth place in his first season at the top table. A year later he was runner-up, only the more experienced Brabham standing between him and the crown. After his friend and mentor left in 1962 to establish his own outfit, McLaren became Cooper's No 1 driver. At the end of the 1965 season, by which time he had slipped down the rankings, McLaren, too, decided to strike out on his own. He had established Bruce McLaren Motor Racing Ltd in 1963 and already won the Tasman Series. He was victorious at Le Mans in 1966, too, but F1 success under his own banner was a longer haul. The breakthrough came in 1968 and the arrival of Cosworth power, which fired McLaren to his fourth victory – the team's maiden win – at the Belgian GP. Teammate Denny Hulme added two more to give McLaren second place in the Constructors' Championship.

Solid scoring put McLaren third in the 1969 title race. He had contested three rounds of the 1970 championship when he was killed at Goodwood while testing for the CanAm series, which McLarens had dominated. His name lives on in one motor racing's iconic marques, whose cars have carried the likes of Lauda, Prost and Senna to championship glory.

Below: Bruce McLaren in his Cosworth-powered McLaren M7A at the United States GP, Watkins Glen, 1968. The team took second place in the Constructors' Championship that season.

Opposite: At the wheel in 1970.

Thurman Munson

YANKEES' CAPTAIN FANTASTIC
7 JUNE 1947 – 2 AUGUST 1979

**Catcher supreme Thurman Munson joined a mediocre New York Yankees team in 1968.
The glory days returned under his inspirational leadership, Munson joining the likes of
Babe Ruth, Lou Gehrig and Joe DiMaggio as one of the Yankees' all-time greats.**

Akron, Ohio, was the birthplace of a baseball legend.
Thurman Munson was a good all-round athlete but
focused on baseball during his time at Kent State

University. In his senior year he made the all-American
college team, earning a reputation that prompted the
Yankees to sign him in the draft in 1968.

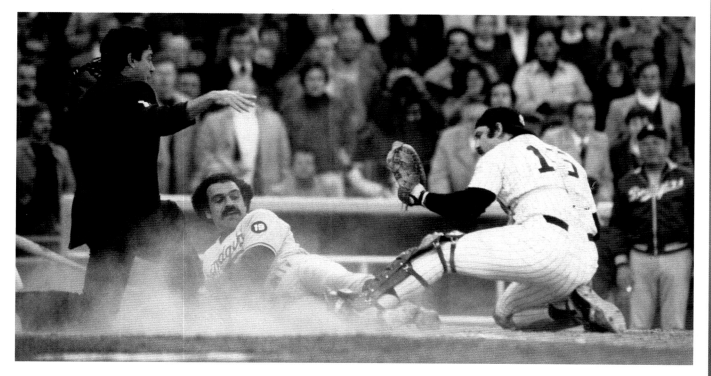

Within two years his performances brought him the American League Rookie of the Year award. Twice in his first four seasons he topped the .300 batting mark and, having quickly made the position of catcher his own, went on to win three consecutive Gold Glove awards.

Following George Steinbrenner's acquisition of the Yankees in 1973, new talent was brought in with a view to competing for top honours. But Munson was the heartbeat of the team. He was a born winner with strong leadership qualities. That was recognized when Munson was handed the captaincy in 1976. It was in many ways an honorary title, a position that had been left vacant since Lou Gehrig left the stage in 1939. Munson carried on in the same vein, leading by example. 1976 was his best year to date: .302 average and 105 RBIs (runs batted in), a performance that brought him the coveted Most Valuable Player (MVP) award.

Munson played a key role as the Yankees' claimed three consecutive American League pennants. He starred in the World Series match against the Cincinatti Reds in 1976, a small personal consolation in a heavy defeat. In both of the next two years the Yankees overcame the LA Dodgers, their first World Series victories since 1962.

Munson gained his pilot's licence so that he could spend as much time as possible with his family in Canton, Ohio. However, on 2 August 1979 during testing of his twin-engined Cessna, the aircraft crashed

'I like the good batting average, but what I do every day behind the plate is a lot more important because it touches so many more people and so many more aspects of the game.'

while attempting to land at Akron-Canton Airport. Thirty-two-year-old Munson survived the impact but was trapped as the plane burst into flames.

The outpouring during the valedictory speeches at the next Yankees game was reminiscent of the emotional scenes 40 years earlier when Gehrig spoke after news broke of his terminal illness; but this time the crowd erupted into spontaneous applause, rather than the customary solemn silence. The Yankees retired the No 15 uniform in his honour.

Opposite: Munson poses for a portrait in the Yankee Stadium, circa 1969.

Above: Munson is late with the tag as Davey Lopes of the Los Angeles Dodgers slides in safe at home plate during the World Series, October 1977.

Ayrton Senna

MOTOR-RACING MAESTRO
21 MARCH 1960 – 1 MAY 1994

Comparing sporting greats across the ages is an impossible task, but for many motor racing fans Ayrton Senna stood apart from the rest. Prodigious natural talent and an extraordinary will to win helped create an aura of invincibility, such that even in a high-risk sport his death was greeted with bewildered incomprehension.

Growing up in a prosperous suburb of São Paulo, the young Senna was drawn to motor cars at an early age, and once he took up karting showed he had aptitude to match his interest. Brazil had its first world champion, Emerson Fittipaldi, the year he turned 12, and emulating that achievement soon became the focus of Senna's life. After becoming the national karting champion and coming close to taking the world crown, Senna stepped up to Formula Ford in 1981 with the British-based Van Diemen team. Two years later it was up the ranks to Formula Three, where he had a season-long tussle with British hope Martin Brundle before clinching the title in the final round. The premier class now beckoned for the hottest young driver on the circuit. Senna tested for Brabham, which didn't go down well with the team's Brazilian top dog Nelson Piquet, and ended up signing for the smaller Toleman outfit. There was early frustration as the mechanical tools he was handed weren't up to the job. But there were glimmers of what was to come, most memorably at Monaco, where he was bearing down on race leader Alain Prost when bad weather brought it to a premature end. Second place from 13th on the grid in a second-rank car was some achievement, but Senna wanted much more. That meant a move to a more competitive team, and a buyout clause in his contract facilitated a move to Lotus. He was soon on top of the podium, scoring his maiden win at the 1985 Portuguese Grand Prix and also taking the chequered flag at Spa.

After three top-four finishes in the Drivers' Championship – two of those won by Alain Prost for McLaren – Senna joined that team in 1988. He and Prost didn't hit it off and a long-running, bitter rivalry set in. Senna bagged eight victories in claiming his first world crown, beating Prost by three points. Those positions were reversed in 1989, a season in which Senna was dogged by mechanical failure. Even with ill luck he was still in with an outside chance of retaining the title with two races left. The first of those was the Japanese GP at Suzuka, where he and Prost tangled and went off the track. Senna rejoined the race and crossed the line first, only to be disqualified. The championship was gone, but there was the consolation of breaking Jim Clark's

Top: In the lead at Monaco in 1993.

Right: Senna celebrates winning the Brazilian GP in 1991.

Opposite: Pre-season testing, Imola, 1991.

record of 33 pole positions. That number would rise to an astonishing 65 by the time of his death.

Prost decamped to Ferrari for the 1990 campaign, adding extra spice to the competition. Senna gained his revenge in yet another two-horse race, with Japan again the scene of a controversial incident. The first-corner spat put both drivers out, and left the Brazilian with an unassailable championship lead. He later admitted to engineering the crash, showing that his skill behind the wheel was backed up by a ruthless winning mentality.

'Being second is to be the first of the ones who lose.'

Senna made it three titles in four years in 1991, beating the two Williams cars. Williams took over as the class act on the grid, while McLaren suffered from the loss of Honda as their engine supplier. Senna still managed five wins and the runner-up spot in 1993, behind his wily old adversary Prost, who had joined

Williams for a swansong season. One of those victories came at Monaco, a record fifth consecutive win on the famous street circuit.

Senna took Prost's seat at Williams in 1994. He headed the grid in the first two races, but failed to finish in either. Next up was the San Marino GP at Imola, where Senna had already notched three wins. The signs were good for victory number four as he

Opposite above: Senna and Prost walk back to the pits after their crash at the start of the Japanese GP in 1990.

Opposite below: Senna and rival Prost share the podium in Adelaide in 1993.

Below: Senna sips a drink before the start of the fatal race at Imola, May 1994.

again put his Williams on pole. As the action restarted following an early accident, Senna's car hit a concrete wall at Tamburello curve. It was a huge impact, but one he might have survived had part of the suspension not flown off and delivered a fatal blow to the head.

Senna had won 41 of his 161 races, a remarkable ratio given that he was by no means always in the best car. And although Michael Schumacher eventually overhauled his record for most pole positions, it was over a much longer time span. Statistics can often paint a false picture, especially in a sport where man and machine are operating in tandem. Perhaps a better indication of Senna's gifts was the 2009 poll of past and present racing drivers, which voted Senna the greatest of them all.

Payne Stewart

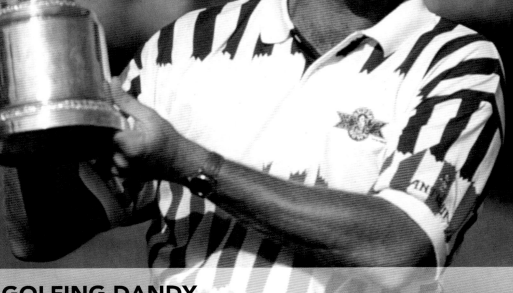

GOLFING DANDY
30 JANUARY 1957 – 25 OCTOBER 1999

Sporting his trademark plus fours and tam-o'-shanter, Payne Stewart looked like a throwback to a bygone era. Behind the extrovert styling and impish sense of fun lay a battle-hardened competitor who won three majors.

William Payne Stewart was born in Springfield, Missouri, the son of a fine amateur player who taught him the rudiments of the game. After graduating from Dallas's Southern Methodist University with a business degree in 1979, the ebullient Stewart turned pro and headed off to play on the Asian circuit. It was part of a learning curve that eventually led to a PGA Tour card in 1982, but it also brought personal fulfilment as he met his future bride.

He won the first of his 11 PGA titles in 1982. After a succession of second places, he won the 1987 Bay Hill Classic, donating the $108,000 prize money to a Florida hospital in memory of his father, who had died two years earlier.

A magnificent late charge at the 1989 PGA Championship, staged at Kemper Lakes, Illinois, brought Stewart his first major. He had trailed Mike Reid by six strokes going into the final round. Two years later, he beat Scott Simpson in an 18-hole play-off to claim the US Open title at Hazeltine, again profiting from a late surge.

Stewart admitted to losing his way for a while, but regained his focus to provide one of golf's enduring images at Pinehurst's No 2 Course in 1999. The 15-foot putt he sank to beat Phil Mickelson and land his second US Open banished all thoughts of the previous year, when he'd added to his tally of runner-up finishes. The one-legged, clenched-fist pose he struck was immortalized in bronze.

'If at the end of the day you can't shake hands with your opponents and still be friends, then you've missed the point.'

In October that year Stewart rejoined Ryder Cup battle at Brookline, his fifth appearance in the competition but first since 1993. With a US victory assured, he graciously conceded his singles match with Colin Montgomerie on the final green.

Within weeks of that triumph, Stewart was killed during a flight from Orlando to Dallas. The private Learjet he was travelling in suffered a catastrophic depressurization, rendering all on board unconscious. It continued on autopilot, crashing in a South Dakota field when its fuel was spent.

One of the game's most colourful characters is remembered with an annual award bearing his name, given to a player who respects the game's traditions and proves himself credit worthy in terms of dress and conduct.

Top: Stewart checks the line of his putt during the US Open, 1991.

Right: The final day singles of the Ryder Cup at Kiawah Island, South Carolina, in 1991.

Opposite: Stewart holds the trophy aloft after winning the US Open at Hazeltine National Golf Club in Minneapolis, Minnesota, 1991.

Music Makers
Classical & Country Music

Bix Beiderbecke

JAZZ AGE GIANT
10 MARCH 1903 – 6 AUGUST 1931

Bix Beiderbecke was a pianist and composer as well as a cornettist nonpareil. In the golden age of jazz he was one of the few white performers to be lauded by black musicians.

One of Leon 'Bix' Beiderbecke's best-known compositions is 'Davenport Blues', titled after his home town in Iowa. If such music is born out of anguish, Bix had sufficient inspiration, for his musical leanings

> 'One of the things I like about jazz is I don't know what's going to happen next.'

caused something of a rift with his middle-class parents. It's said that one of the reasons he was shipped off to Lake Forest Academy in Illinois was to wean him off jazz. It didn't work. He was expelled from that institution – his fondness for alcohol already apparent – and followed his calling. Even when he was a recording artist playing

Below: Bix Beiderbecke (far right) poses with his band, The Wolverines.

Opposite: Bix poses with his cornet circa 1925.

with some of the country's top bands, it cut little ice with his parents. On one recuperative visit home he found records he'd sent home stashed away, unplayed.

Beiderbecke was largely self-taught and struggled to sight-read. He used unorthodox fingering when playing the cornet, and some said his untutored style was the key to his originality. One contemporary described the sound he achieved as 'like shooting bullets at a bell'. After hearing Bix play, Louis Armstrong said: 'Those pretty notes went right through me.' They were able to play together in private, but in an age of segregation couldn't record or perform in tandem.

Bix came to prominence in 1924 playing with The Wolverines, his solos embellishing some highly influential recordings, such as 'Jazz Me Blues'. He went on to play with Jean Goldkette's dance band,

one of the top white orchestras in the country, and in 1927 joined 'King of Jazz' Paul Whiteman's outfit. Between assignments Bix played and recorded with other ensembles, often with saxophonist Frank Trumbauer. 'I'm Coming, Virginia' and 'Singin' the Blues' date from this period and show off his melodic inventiveness.

His drinking out of control, Bix left Whiteman in September 1929. His health was such that he would miss cues, sometimes entire performances. One score was said to carry the inscription, 'Wake up Bix'. Hopes that he would recover and rejoin the band were never realized. Beiderbecke's dissolute lifestyle hastened his death, aged 28, in an insalubrious New York apartment. Little known beyond jazz circles when he died, Bix later assumed legendary status. Louis Armstrong said many tried to imitate his style; none succeeded.

Jacques Brel

POPULAR SINGER OF FRENCH SONGS
8 APRIL 1929 – 9 OCTOBER 1978

Jacques Brel wrote and sang emotional songs that moved audiences to tears. He is one of the most popular singers in the French language, still selling thousands of albums more than 30 years after his death.

Many of Brel's fans assume he was French, but Jacques Romain Georges Brel was born and brought up in Belgium. Brel was to join the family packaging business, but showed no interest or aptitude for office work. Instead he began writing and performing songs, despite his family's disapproval. In 1953 he made his first recording, and a talent spotter for the Philips label invited him to Paris. Although he had a wife and two small children, Brel left them behind and went to work in France.

At first he found it hard to break into the performance circuit, but by 1955 his wife and family were able to join him in Paris. In 1957 his second album brought him real recognition, when the title song, 'Quand on n'a que l'amour', became a hit. Other albums followed and Brel went on an extensive series of tours over the next few years that soon brought him to the brink of international stardom. Meanwhile his family returned to Belgium, and Brel embarked on a series of affairs, apparently with his wife's acceptance.

Above: Jacques Brel enjoys singing backstage at Olympia, Paris, circa 1958.

Right: Brel visits the Cannes Film Festival in May 1972.

Opposite: Watching the world go by, circa 1970.

'To be bourgeois is to have a certain type of materialism... It's a type of mediocrity of the spirit. It's everything I dislike.'

Brel's songs were written to be performed rather than simply sung; he explored complex themes of love and loss, religion and society. His love-hate relationship with his home country led him to write 'Le plat pays', a moving tribute to the low skies and melancholy beauty of the Belgian landscape, but also 'Les Flamandes', which depicts Flemish women in an unflattering light.

In 1966 Brel decided to stop singing and gave a series of emotional farewell concerts. Instead he turned to acting, performing successfully in a series of plays and films over the next few years. In 1974 he bought a yacht, which he sailed to the Marquesas Islands – where he decided to stay. Not long afterwards he was diagnosed with lung cancer and knew he did not have long to live. He returned to Paris to record a new album in 1977, with material written in the Marquesas Islands; over a million copies were pre-ordered before its release. He returned to France again the following year when his health declined; he died in Paris but was buried in the Marquesas.

Maria Callas

'LA DIVINA'
2 DECEMBER 1923 – 16 SEPTEMBER 1977

Her voice divided opinion, but her singing and acting talents combined made Maria Callas the most celebrated diva of the 20th century.

Maria Kalogeropoulou was born in New York to Greek immigrant parents, who later shortened the family name to the more manageable Callas. Maria was something of a singing prodigy, and in 1937 her mother Evangelia returned to her homeland with Maria and her sister in order to further her musical training. Callas studied at the Athens Conservatoire and counted among her teachers Elvira de Hidalgo, one of the great sopranos of the 1920s.

She made her professional debut in 1940 and forged a reputation with the Athens Opera during the war years. Her career took off when she returned to America, impressing the tenor Giovanni Zenatello enough to earn an engagement at the Arena in Verona, performing in Ponchielli's *La Gioconda*. She also found romance in the shape of Italian industrialist Giovanni Battista Meneghini, whom she married in 1949.

The conductor at her Italian debut in Verona was Tullio Serafin, who immediately recognized her potential. Later, when opera buffs argued about the quality of her voice, Serafin said he regarded it as the most beautiful sound he had ever heard because it was always true. With Serafin's backing, Callas was engaged to play Isolde, the Irish princess of Wagner's *Tristan und Isolde*, and the title role in Puccini's *Turandot*. Her performances in these, and as Aida and Brünnhilde, showed her mastery of the heavy dramatic roles. She left the operatic world agape in 1949 when she took over the role of Elvira in Bellini's *I Puritani* a mere week after singing Brünnhilde in *Die Walküre*. Callas showed in spectacular style that her talent spanned the great heroic roles and the more colourful heroines to be found in the work of bel canto masters Bellini, Donizetti and Rossini. Over time she focused on the latter, and indeed was instrumental in the revival of bel canto opera in the post-war period.

Top: Callas performed and recorded with tenor Giuseppe di Stefano on several occasions.

Right: With Aristotle Onassis, 1961.

Opposite: Callas's remarkable musical and dramatic talents led to her being hailed as La Divina.

In particular Maria Callas was famed for the title roles in Bellini's *Norma*, Cherubini's *Medea* and Donizetti's *Anna Bolena* and *Lucia di Lammermoor*. Early and middle-period Verdi operas were also added to her repertoire. Gilda and Violetta, from *Rigoletto* and *La Traviata*, respectively, were among the roles she made her own. Reviewing a performance of the latter at London's Covent Garden in 1958, one critic waxed lyrical over her voice: 'In its control for the shaping of a phrase, in its incredibly smooth legato, in its unerring use of the dangerous portamento, in its placing of the words on the tone, in the beauty of singing mezzo voce and sotto voce, hers is the art of singing at its highest.'

'First I lost my voice, then I lost my figure and then I lost Onassis.'

Rudolf Bing, who ran New York's Metropolitan Opera House for over 20 years and had several run-ins with the temperamental star, spent years trying to bring her to the city of her birth to perform. He found that Callas could be as abrasive and confrontational off stage as Tosca – another signature role – was in her dealings with Baron Scarpia. 'I would like to be Maria,' she said with solipsistic grandeur, 'but there is La Callas who demands that I carry myself with her dignity.' Bing could only look on as Callas made her American debut at Chicago's Lyric Opera, which secured her services for the 1954 and 1955 seasons. He was not blind to her technical flaws, yet he described her 1956 New York debut as 'undoubtedly the most exciting of all such in my time at the Metropolitan'. He went further: 'I never fully enjoyed any other artist in one of her roles after she did it.'

Many column inches were devoted to Callas's private life. Her appearance changed dramatically in the early 1950s as she shed around 60 lb, the portly performer transformed into a svelte, glamorous opera star. Her marriage unravelled in 1959 as she embarked on an affair with shipping tycoon Aristotle Onassis. The divorce proceedings were a long-running soap opera, Callas renouncing her US citizenship in 1966 in an attempt to expedite matters. By the time the divorce came through, Onassis had married Jacqueline Kennedy.

When Maria Callas was found dead in her Paris apartment, aged 53, over a decade had passed since her last appearance on the operatic stage. She hadn't retired completely. There was a non-singing role in Pier Paolo Pasolini's *Medea* in 1969 and an international recital tour with the tenor Giuseppe di Stefano in 1974, her final public performances.

As a singer Callas may not have been the equal of her contemporary Joan Sutherland. Critics pointed to a brittle, metallic quality in her voice, an uncertainty in the high register and excessive vibrato. But her acting prowess, her interpretative gifts, her sheer theatricality more than compensated for any vocal imperfection, and made Callas one of opera's most electrifying performers.

Above: In the role of Norma at the Metropolitan Opera House, New York, 1956.

Opposite: Callas and Italian tenor Renato Cioni in a scene from Tosca *at Covent Garden, London, 1964.*

Patsy Cline

COUNTRY LEGEND
8 SEPTEMBER 1932 – 5 MARCH 1963

In the brief period she enjoyed at the top, Patsy Cline carved her name high up in the roll-call of country music greats. She was a crossover artist who had mainstream pop success while establishing herself as a Nashville legend.

Virginia Patterson Hensley grew up in Winchester in the state of Virginia, where she showed a flair for performing at an early age. She taught herself to dance and play the piano, and soon set her sights on making it as a country singer. She maintained that after recovering from a childhood throat infection her voice 'boomed like Kate Smith's' – a reference to a powerhouse chanteuse who was enormously popular in the 1940s.

> '*Carnegie Hall was real fabulous, but you know, it ain't as big as the Grand Ole Opry.*'

At 14 she impressed Joltin' Jim McCoy and the Melody Playboys enough to secure a spot on their local radio show. She made similarly successful overtures to Grand Ole Opry star Wally Fowler, and in 1954 landed a record deal with the minor, Pasadena-based Four-Star label. By then she had taken to the stage as Patsy Cline. Bandleader and mentor Bill Peer, who engaged her as a vocalist and brokered the Four-Star deal, thought 'Patsy' fitted the bill better than 'Virginia', while a whirlwind, short-lived marriage to Gerald Cline provided the surname.

Cline's early recordings failed to provide the breakthrough, and she was unenthusiastic about releasing 'Walkin' After Midnight', which became one of her biggest hits. After performing the song on *Arthur Godfrey's Talent Scouts* TV show in January 1957, it made No 2 in the country list and broke the Top 20 in the pop charts. A follow-up hit proved elusive, perhaps because of the strictures imposed by her contract. Those disappeared after she signed to Decca in 1960, the year she also joined the cast of the Grand Ole Opry. 'I Fall to Pieces' hit the top of the country charts, and while her rendition of Willie Nelson's 'Crazy' peaked at No 2, it became her signature number. In 1962 'She's Got You' gave her another country chart-topper and became her first recording to break the UK Top 50.

On 5 March 1963, with 'Leaving on Your Mind' featuring in both charts, Patsy Cline was killed when the plane carrying her from a benefit performance in Kansas City back to her Nashville home went down in bad weather near Camden, Tennessee. A decade later, she became the first solo female artist to be inducted into the Country Music Hall of Fame.

Opposite and right: Studio portraits of Patsy Cline. Decca used the image on the right on the sleeve of the 1962 album Sentimentally Yours.

Nat King Cole

JAZZ PIANIST AND SINGER
17 MARCH 1919 – 15 FEBRUARY 1965

Nat 'King' Cole is best known for his warm baritone voice, which took songs such as rhythm 'n' blues standard '(Get Your Kicks On) Route 66' and later ballads such as 'Unforgettable' storming into the charts. However, he was also a celebrated jazz pianist and is credited with being a major influence in the development of rock 'n' roll.

According to legend Cole only began to sing after an inebriated customer requested 'Sweet Lorraine' during their set; Cole later said the story wasn't true since he often sang between instrumental pieces – but that he had begun to sing more only because people requested it. The trio signed with new label

'I'm a musician at heart, I know I'm not really a singer... But I sing because the public buys it.'

Nathaniel Adams Coles was born in Montgomery, Alabama, and christened Nat 'King' Cole by a Los Angeles club owner in 1937. He formed The King Cole Trio – Cole on piano, Oscar Moore on guitar and Wesley Price on double bass – in the late 1930s; the line-up was regarded as innovative because there was no drummer. No less an authority than Count Basie marvelled at the trio's improvisational interplay: 'Those cats used to read each other's minds – it was unbelievable.'

Above: The Nat King Cole Trio: guitarist Oscar Moore (left), Nat King Cole (front) and Johnny Miller (right), who took over on double bass in the 1940s .

Right: Cole with his wife Maria at the Coconut Grove in Hollywood, 1964.

Opposite: Cole poses in front of a piano, circa 1954.

Capitol Records in 1943, and went on to become so successful that the new Capitol Records HQ that was completed in 1956 quickly became known as 'the house that Nat built'.

Cole made television history in 1956, when he became the first African American to front his own TV show, on NBC-TV. Despite support from many contemporary artists the show failed to gain nationwide sponsorship and was pulled after just over a year. Although this might partly have been due to racism, even Frank Sinatra's show failed to draw a large audience around the same time. Cole himself had refused to accept racism throughout his life, avoiding segregated venues and declining to work in the South after being attacked on stage during a concert in Birmingham, Alabama.

During his career Cole had been a very heavy smoker; at the time smoking was not considered dangerous and he believed it gave his voice its distinctive rich tone. In the early 1960s the years of inhaling smoke finally took their toll; he died of lung cancer in 1965 in Santa Monica, California. His work has remained popular – a tribute album released in 1991, which included a version of 'Unforgettable' in which daughter Natalie's voice was added to her father's, went on to win seven Grammy awards.

John Coltrane

AVANT-GARDE JAZZ SAXOPHONIST
23 SEPTEMBER 1926 – 17 JULY 1967

Saxophonist John Coltrane was one of the most important and influential figures in the history of jazz. Although there is controversy about some of his work, he was at the forefront of the development of free form jazz and inspired other musicians to experiment.

Born in North Carolina, John William Coltrane was always surrounded by music; his father was an amateur musician who played several instruments. Coltrane began playing clarinet and alto horn in a community band, but later switched to alto saxophone. After briefly attending the Ornstein School of Music he was drafted into the US Navy during World War II and performed with the navy jazz band in Hawaii.

After the war Coltrane began playing tenor saxophone with the Eddie Vinson Band, which introduced him to different playing styles. During this period he worked with several other bands and his passion for experimentation developed. In 1955 he was hired by the Miles Davis Quintet, which led to extensive recordings – not only with the quintet but also as sideman for other bands. After Coltrane became famous, many of these sideman recordings were re-released under his name. He developed a method of playing several notes together and released a couple of albums under his own name, with a varied line-up each time, as well as still recording with Davis.

'My music is the spiritual expression of what I am.'

In 1959 Coltrane worked with Davis on *Kind of Blue*, a landmark album featuring improvisations based on scales that became one of the best-selling albums in jazz history. The following year he formed the John Coltrane Quartet and began to create his own innovative and expressive music. One of the quartet's most famous albums, *A Love Supreme*, celebrates the power, glory and love of God; Coltrane had struggled with drug addition for many years, and many believe his spirituality developed after a near overdose. Despite its religious content, the album was a commercial success.

From 1965 Coltrane became interested in avant-garde jazz, and his playing became freer and more abstract, inspiring his band to follow his lead. However, later two of the original members left as other free musicians began to play with Coltrane more regularly, taking the music in very experimental directions. In 1967 Coltrane died suddenly of liver cancer, leaving a large amount of recorded material for release over the following years. He won several Grammys and a Pulitzer Prize Special Citation after his death and was also canonized as a saint by the African Orthodox Church.

Left: Coltrane pioneered the development of free jazz.

Opposite: As his career progressed, Coltrane and his music took on an increasingly spiritual dimension.

Sam Cooke

SOUL LEGEND
22 JANUARY 1931 – 11 DECEMBER 1964

One of the most influential black artists in history, Sam Cooke made the transition from gospel singer to pop star. He is lauded as a seminal figure in the development of soul and R & B.

He was born Samuel Cook in Clarksdale, Mississippi, his Baptist minister father moving the family to Chicago when he was two. From an early age Sam sang spirituals with his siblings, providing a musical interlude to their father's preaching rounds. In his teens he performed with The Highway QCs, and in 1950 joined The Soul Stirrers, one of the pre-eminent gospel groups of the day. With songs such as 'Jesus Gave Me Water', The Soul Stirrers successfully worked 'the gospel highway' circuit. Cooke's sweet, smooth vocals, good looks and easy charm won him hordes of female fans, but he was a big fish in a small pond, something the ambitious singer-songwriter wanted to address by entering the secular mainstream. Such music was anathema to the gospel set, and Cooke risked alienation by performing songs devoid of spiritual content.

'It's been a long time coming, but I know a change gonna come.'

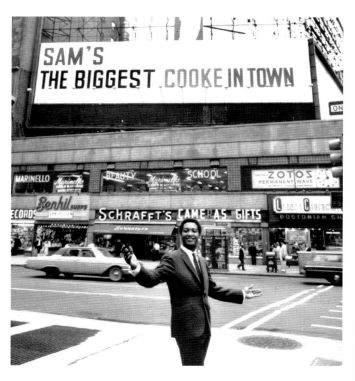

Above: Sam Cooke joined The Soul Stirrers in 1950.

Top: Cooke poses in front of a billboard advertising his show.

Opposite: Cooke in the studio.

Working with producer Robert Blackwell, who recognized his crossover potential, Cooke released 'Lovable' in January 1957. A reworked version of a Soul Stirrers' number, it went out under the name of Dale Cook. Few were fooled.

Cooke laid his cards on the table by quitting The Soul Stirrers in May 1957. If he lost any fans, he replaced them many times over as 'You Send Me' became one of biggest hits of the year. Follow-up successes included 'Only Sixteen', 'Wonderful World' and 'Chain Gang', the last of those his first hit after signing to RCA in 1960. The sure-fire run continued with 'Cupid' ,'Twistin' the Night Away' and 'Another Saturday Night'.

Cooke had business acumen to match his singing and composing talent, establishing his own publishing company and label. Along with frothy dance-craze songs, such as 'Everybody Likes to Cha Cha Cha', there were meatier offerings, not least the Dylan-inspired 'A Change is Gonna Come', a civil rights anthem referenced by Barack Obama in his 2008 victory speech. Cooke was out on the town in LA when that song was being pressed as the B-side of his latest single 'Shake'. The revelry ended at a downmarket motel, where he was shot following an altercation with the manager. The events remain shrouded in mystery but did nothing to diminish the reputation of an artist who paved the way for gospel performers, such as Aretha Franklin and Marvin Gaye, to become 1960s soul sensations.

Jacqueline du Pré

LEGENDARY CELLIST
26 JANUARY 1945 – 19 OCTOBER 1987

Jacqueline du Pré is acknowledged as one of the greatest talents ever to play the cello; she combined mind, body and soul to produce the most expressive music, playing with great precision and purity of tone.

By the age of ten du Pré was studying under cellist William Pleeth, and later she also studied with celebrated musicians Casals, Tortelier and Rostropovich. At 11 she became the youngest recipient of the Guilhermina Suggia Award and at 15 was awarded the Gold Medal of the Guildhall School of Music. By the time she was 16 she had begun playing professionally, and in 1962 she

Left: A young du Pré performs in January 1962.

Below: Golden couple Jacqueline du Pré and her husband pianist and conductor Daniel Barenboim pictured in 1967.

Opposite: On stage in London, 1968.

'Playing lifts you out of yourself into a delirious place.'

Born in Oxford, England, du Pré came from a musical family; her mother was a fine pianist and gifted teacher and her older sister Hilary later became a flautist. Her father was editor of *The Accountant*; the French-sounding surname came from his Channel Island ancestry. Just before her fifth birthday, when she was already showing musical promise, du Pré apparently heard the sound of a cello on the radio and asked her mother if she could learn to play.

performed Elgar's *Cello Concerto* for the first time at the Royal Festival Hall with the BBC Symphony Orchestra under Rudolf Schwarz. The following year she performed the same work at the BBC Proms; it was so popular she was invited back three years in succession. Her 1965 recording of Elgar's *Cello Concerto*, with Sir John Barbirolli and the London Symphony Orchestra, established her as an international star. She was also a brilliant chamber-music player, collaborating with many of the greatest names in music, such as violinists Yehudi Menuhin and Itzhak Perlman and pianist Daniel Barenboim. In 1967 du Pré married Barenboim in Jerusalem,

although she later had an affair with conductor Christopher Finzi – who was married to her sister.

At some point in 1971 du Pré started losing feeling in her fingers and her arms 'felt like lead'. Her playing began to deteriorate and between 1971 and 1972 she rarely performed. By October 1973 she had been diagnosed with multiple sclerosis, but resumed playing for one last tour; by this time she had lost sensation in her fingers and sometimes experienced difficulty in judging the weight of the bow. After 1973 du Pré no longer performed, although she taught occasionally. Her health continued to deteriorate and she died in London in 1987.

George Gershwin

POPULAR COMPOSER
26 SEPTEMBER 1898 – 11 JULY 1937

George Gershwin remains one of America's most beloved popular musicians, composer of such classics as *Rhapsody in Blue*, Broadway musicals such as *Funny Face* and original film scores for several Hollywood movies, including *Shall We Dance*, starring Fred Astaire and Ginger Rogers.

Born Jacob Gershowitz in Brooklyn in 1898, Gershwin was the second child of a close-knit Russian immigrant family. He began his musical career as a song-plugger on Tin Pan Alley and his first published song earned him five dollars – a third of his weekly salary at the time. After he began working with young lyricist Irving Caesar in 1919 they composed a number of hit songs including 'Swanee', which sold more than a million copies. Over the course of the next four years Gershwin wrote more than 40 songs, as well as a 25-minute opera, *Blue Monday*, in collaboration with lyricist Buddy DeSylva.

In 1924 Gershwin collaborated with his older brother, lyricist Ira, on the musical comedy *Lady Be Good*, which introduced classic songs such as 'Fascinating Rhythm' and 'The Man I Love'. It was the beginning of a partnership that would continue for the rest of Gershwin's life, but while still continuing to compose popular music for the stage he was also trying to make his mark as a serious composer. It was also in 1924 that his jazz-influenced *Rhapsody in Blue* premiered in New York's Aeolian Hall. Gershwin followed this success with the orchestral works *Piano Concerto in F*, *Rhapsody No 2* and *An American in Paris*. Some serious music critics dismissed Gershwin's classical work as banal, but it was always popular with the audience.

'Life is a lot like jazz... it's best when you improvise.'

In 1931 the Gershwin brothers wrote *Of Thee I Sing*, a musical lampooning American politics, which in 1932 became the first musical to win the Pulitzer Prize for Drama. George also dealt with other social issues in music: *Porgy and Bess*, a 'folk opera' based on African-American life with a cast of classically-trained African-American singers, was not initially widely accepted although it later came to be seen as an important piece in American operatic history. One of the most famous songs from it, 'Summertime' has become a jazz classic and exists in more than 2,500 different versions. In 1937, after many successes on Broadway, the Gershwin brothers went to Hollywood. Not long after arriving George became ill and was diagnosed as having a brain tumour; although surgeons operated to remove the tumour, he died following the surgery.

Below: George Gershwin annotates the sheet music for the film Delicious *(1931) while his brother and partner, lyricist Ira Gershwin (left), and British dramatist Guy Bolton look on.*

Opposite: Gershwin at work, circa 1930.

207

Billie Holiday

'LADY DAY'
7 APRIL 1915 – 17 JULY 1959

Despite her lack of technical training, Billie Holiday's unique diction, inimitable phrasing and dramatic intensity made her the outstanding jazz singer of her day; her poignant voice is still considered one of the greatest jazz voices of all time. She is remembered today both for her innovative improvisation techniques and her signature moving ballads.

Born Eleanora Fagan in Philadelphia, Pennsylvania, Holiday grew up in the jazz centre of Baltimore, but later moved to New York where she sang in Harlem nightclubs, taking her professional name from screen star Billie Dove and musician Clarence Holiday, her absent father. Although she never learned to read music, Holiday quickly became an active part of one of the most vibrant jazz scenes in the country. At 18 she was spotted by John Hammond and cut her first record with Benny Goodman, then on the verge of fame. Two years later she recorded four songs that became hits, including 'What a Little Moonlight Can Do' and 'Miss Brown to You', which landed her a recording contract of her own. She often worked with tenor saxophonist Lester Young, who gave her the nickname Lady Day. She joined Count Basie in 1937 and then Artie Shaw in 1938, one of the first black women to work with a white orchestra, an impressive accomplishment at the time.

Holiday's soulful singing voice and her ability to make any material her own made her a superstar; white gardenias, worn in her hair, became a trademark.

In the 1930s, when she was working with Columbia Records, she discovered the poem 'Strange Fruit', an emotional piece about the lynching of a black man. Since Columbia would not allow her to record it, she released the song with Commodore, and it became one of her classics.

In her personal life, Holiday's romances were often destructive and abusive. She married James Monroe in 1941; already a drinker, Holiday soon picked up her new husband's opium habit. They later divorced, but another boyfriend, trumpeter Joe Guy, introduced her to heroin. By the early 1950s her heavy drinking and drug use had begun to affect her health. Holiday gave her final performance in New York City on 25 May 1959 and not long afterwards was admitted to hospital with heart and liver problems. She was arrested for possession of drugs while still in her hospital bed, but died from cirrhosis of the liver before the case came to court.

'I never hurt nobody but myself and that's nobody's business but my own.'

Top: Holiday rests after a performance, 1954.

Left: At the microphone wearing her trademark gardenias.

Opposite: Billie Holiday sings in a nightclub, circa 1954.

Mario Lanza

'VOICE OF THE CENTURY'
31 JANUARY 1921 – 7 OCTOBER 1959

Mario Lanza was the world's foremost tenor in the 1950s. The inheritor of
Enrico Caruso's mantle inspired the likes of Pavarotti, Domingo and Carreras.

Alfred Arnold Cocozza was born in Philadelphia to Italian immigrant parents. Freddie, as he was known, grew up listening to Caruso records, to which he would sing along. Recognizing his talent, father Antonio and mother Maria arranged for him to have singing lessons, but the big break came in 1942, when Serge Koussevitsky, conductor of Boston's Symphony Orchestra, granted him a scholarship to the prestigious Berkshire Music Center in Lenox, Massachusetts, home of the Tanglewood Music Festival, where the BSO performed every summer. Taking his stage name from his mother, who was born Maria Lanza, he was an instant hit in the role of Fenton in *The Merry Wives of Windsor*, and continued to perform during his three years of military service. After demobilization Lanza made records, appeared on radio and gave concert performances. In 1948 he took the role of Pinkerton in a production of *Madam Butterfly* staged in New Orleans. It was his sole operatic outing, save for his performance in the *Merry Wives*.

'I sing as though my life depends on it, and if I ever stop doing that, then I'll stop living.'

Lanza signed to MGM after studio head Louis B. Mayer attended a Hollywood Bowl concert in 1947. He made his screen debut in *That Midnight Kiss* (1949), playing a singing truck driver. It was a singing fisherman in the follow-up, *The Toast of New Orleans* (1950), which featured the hit song 'Be My Love'. *The Great Caruso* (1951), a biopic of his hero, was Lanza's personal favourite and included the popular arias 'La donna è mobile' and 'Celeste Aida'.

The movies were usually frothy vehicles whose aim was to showcase Lanza's vocal gifts. One critic said of his 1952 offering *Because You're Mine*: 'The film might have turned itself into a gramophone recital of his records without any appreciable loss.'

A dispute with the studio meant that Lanza featured only on the soundtrack of *The Student Prince* (1954). He had weight and alcohol problems, but returned to make three more films. His final screen appearance was in *For the First Time* (1959), playing a famous tenor whose love interest is deaf.

The alcohol, bingeing and crash-dieting left Lanza in poor health. The man possessed of 'the greatest voice of the 20th century', according to Arturo Toscanini, suffered a fatal heart attack in Rome two years after relocating to the land of his forefathers. He was 38.

Top: Lanza's short career covered opera, radio, concerts, recordings and motion pictures.

Above: Kathryn Grayson and Mario Lanza in That Midnight Kiss.

Opposite: Hollywood columnist Hedda Hopper wrote that Lanza was the 'last of the great romantic performers'.

Charlie Parker

SAXOPHONE VIRTUOSO
29 AUGUST 1920 – 12 MARCH 1955

The Charlie 'Bird' Parker story bears testament to the sad truth that genius and self-destructiveness are common bedfellows. The man who reshaped jazz in the 1940s was also an inveterate drug and alcohol abuser, such that the coroner who examined his raddled, lifeless body estimated him to be in his mid-50s. He was 34.

Parker was raised in Kansas City, taking up the saxophone at school. He dropped out at 14 and started playing with local bands in what was a thriving jazz and blues scene. It was intensely competitive and Parker was determined to excel. He was influenced enormously by the sounds he heard in the New York clubs. Parker first visited the Big Apple in 1939, and although he returned home to hook up with Jay

'If you don't live it, it won't come out of your horn.'

McShann's band – with whom he played on and off for four years – from 1942 New York was his spiritual home. He was a regular on the 52nd Street club scene, where he played with the likes of Dizzy Gillespie and Thelonius Monk. Parker had already made recordings with McShann, playing solo on tracks such as 'Hootie Blues' and 'Confessin' the Blues', and over time he

Left and opposite: Charlie Parker with his saxophone.

Below: Parker plays alongside Charlie Ventura and Buddy De Franco with the Metronome All-Stars in 1949.

developed his unique improvisational style. Parker said he could hear the sound he wanted to achieve long before he could actually play it.

'It' was termed bebop in the mid-1940s, a jazz revolution that alienated some traditionalists, although 12-bar blues invariably underpinned the complex rhythms and melodic patterns that Parker laid on top. His influence went beyond reed players. Other jazz musicians adapted Parker's motifs to their own instruments, while students who avidly deconstructed his solos may have stumbled in trying to adopt his mantra: 'Don't play the saxophone, let it play you'. Charlie Parker secured his place in the history of popular music as an influential innovator and unique stylist.

Compositions such as 'Now's the Time' and 'Ornithology' became standards, but it was as an innovative virtuoso that Parker is remembered. He is also known for his excesses: Parker's appetite for drugs, alcohol and women was as legendary as his playing. Heroin addiction put him in California's state hospital in 1946, a period immortalized in 'Relaxin' at Camarillo'. Drug addiction cost him his cabaret licence in 1951, and there were suicide attempts following the death of his infant daughter in 1953. His gave his final performance a few days before his death at Birdland, the Broadway club named in his honour.

213

Édith Piaf

'LITTLE SPARROW'
19 DECEMBER 1915 – 11 OCTOBER 1963

One of France's greatest singers, Édith Piaf's poignant ballads reflected her tragic story.
Her life was one of sharp contrasts: the powerful voice emanating from a diminutive figure;
the enviable acclaim masking a troubled personal history.

Piaf was born Édith Giovanna Gassion to a street-acrobat father and neglectful café-singer mother. Legend has it she entered the world on the pavement in the working-class Belleville district of Paris, a plaque marking the birth of a singer 'whose voice would later move the world'.

By her mid-teens she was eking out a living as a street singer, which led to her discovery by nightclub owner Louis Leplée. He named her 'la môme piaf' – 'urchin sparrow' – which suited her waifish background and birdlike appearance. It was under the adopted name of Édith Piaf that she captivated music hall and cabaret audiences.

'I want to make people cry even when they don't understand my words.'

Her first big hit came in 1937 with 'Mon légionnaire', while later successes included 'Les trois cloches' and 'La vie en rose'. The latter became a signature number to match her trademark black dress. Piaf sang about life on the street, imperfect love, unsavoury characters; the vicissitudes of life delivered with stoicism, not self-pity.

Her lyrics reflected a life whose turbulence continued into adulthood. One affair produced a daughter who died in infancy. Another lover, boxing champion Marcel Cerdan, was killed in a plane crash. Among numerous dalliances there were two marriages. The first, to singer Jacques Pills, lasted four years. Her second husband, Theophanis Lamboukas (aka Théo Sarapo), was 20 years her junior when they married in 1962. She duetted with the latter on 'A quoi ça sert l'amour? – 'What Use is Love?' – a song full of wryness and optimism recorded a year before her death.

Piaf was dogged by ill health in her latter years. In 1951, at the height of her fame, she suffered injuries in a car accident that led to morphine addiction. This, in tandem with a drinking habit, exacted a heavy toll.

Top: French actor and singer Yves Montand poses with Édith Piaf, whose support was instrumental in his success.

Right: Piaf with boxer Marcel Cerdan. The story of their love affair was told in the film Édith and Marcel in 1983.

Opposite: Piaf performs in the mid-1940s.

She recovered from a long period of illness to make a triumphant return to the stage in 1961, but it was a brief respite. She died from cancer two years later, her funeral procession drawing hundreds of thousands of mourners onto the streets of Paris. Fans the world over took to their hearts a performer whose best known song – 'Non, je ne regrette rien' – encapsulated her outlook on life.

Bessie Smith

EMPRESS OF THE BLUES
15 APRIL 1894 – 26 SEPTEMBER 1937

Bessie Smith was one of the great classic blues singers. Popular with both white and African-American audiences, she soon became the highest-paid black performer of her era and her rendition of 'St Louis Blues' with Louis Armstrong is considered to be one of finest recordings of the 1920s.

Born in Chattanooga, Tennessee, Smith was raised in poverty after her parents died when she was a child. She and brother Andrew began busking the streets of Chattanooga and at 18 Smith joined a travelling show as a dancer. The show also featured blues vocalist Ma Rainey, who encouraged Smith to start singing the blues. Smith later joined the African-American vaudeville circuit and built up a following in the south and along the Eastern Seaboard. In 1923 she made her recording debut on Columbia, accompanied by pianist Clarence Williams; 'Downhearted Blues' sold more than 750,000 copies that same year. With her rich, powerful, clear voice, Smith soon became a successful recording artist and worked with many great jazz musicians of the era, including Fletcher Henderson, James P. Johnson, Coleman Hawkins, Don Redman and Louis Armstrong. She could deliver songs with great emotion, perhaps drawing on an unhappy personal life. Her six-year marriage to Jack Gee was stormy, although she later found happiness with old friend Richard Morgan, and she battled with an alcohol problem throughout much of her career.

'I've been poor and I've been rich, and rich is better.'

By 1931 classic blues had fallen out of style and Columbia dropped Smith from its roster. However, despite having no record company she was still popular in the South and continued to tour, drawing large crowds and beginning to restyle herself as a swing musician. She was on the verge of a comeback when, while being driven by Morgan in Mississippi late at night, her car hit a truck and rolled over crushing her left arm and ribs. Smith was taken to a nearby African-American hospital in Clarksdale, but died of her injuries without regaining consciousness. John Hammond later wrote a magazine article suggesting that Smith had bled to death because she was first taken to a whites-only hospital and refused admission; although this was not true, the rumour persisted. Her funeral was attended by thousands but her estranged husband made sure her

grave remained unmarked, twice pocketing the money raised. In 1970, singer Janis Joplin and Juanita Green, daughter of Bessie's housekeeper, finally arranged to erect a headstone.

Opposite and right: Bessie Smith photographed during the 1920s. It is said that Columbia nicknamed her 'Queen of the Blues', but that a PR-minded person soon upgraded her title to 'Empress'.

Fats Waller

KING OF 'STRIDE'
21 MAY 1904 – 15 DECEMBER 1943

As well as being a master of Harlem 'stride' piano, Fats Waller was a singer, composer and bandleader who also turned his hand to broadcasting and movies. ... an-life character, he remains an enduringly popular jazz musician.

The son of a New York Baptist preacher, Thomas Wright Waller's introduction to the keyboard was playing the church organ. By his mid-teens he was providing accompaniment for silent movies at the city's Lincoln Theater and playing on the vaudeville and club circuit. He was a protégé of James P. Johnson, acknowledged as one of the great exponents of 'stride' piano – so-called because of the distances the left hand covered – but Waller's appeal went far beyond keyboard dexterity. He was a wit and a consummate entertainer who won over hordes of fans with his unique brand of clowning and virtuosity. He also had a gargantuan appetite, which earned him his nickname.

Fats made his recording debut in 1922, 'Wild Cat Blues' and 'Squeeze Me' among his popular early works. He played at bootleg parlors as well as legitimate venues, on one occasion virtually kidnapped to perform for Al Capone, who was a fan. In 1928 he collaborated with James P. Johnson and lyricist Andy Razaf on the all-black musical 'Keep Shufflin''. He struck up a lasting friendship and fertile professional relationship with Razaf, the 1929 Broadway show *Hot Chocolates* among their collaborations. It featured 'Ain't Misbehavin'', probably the song for which Fats is best remembered. 'Honeysuckle Rose' and 'Keepin' Out of Mischief Now' were products of one of the most successful songwriting partnerships of the era. Fats also had big hits with 'I'm

'You get that right tickin' rhythm, man, and it's on!'

Gonna Sit Right Down and Write Myself a Letter' and 'Your Feet's Too Big'.

Waller's fame increased following the formation of his famous Rhythm Band in 1934. He enjoyed huge success both on disc and on tour in the last decade of his life. Fats visited Europe twice in the late 1930s, performing at the London Palladium and even being allowed to try out the organ at Notre Dame Cathedral in Paris. There were also screen appearances in *Hooray for Love* (1935), *King of Burlesque* (1936) and *Stormy Weather* (1943), Fats performing 'Ain't Misbehavin'' in the last of those.

Waller lived a life of excess, an alimony battle adding to the strains upon him. He was travelling by rail from the West Coast to New York when he died, succumbing to pneumonia during a stopover in Kansas City.

Opposite: Fats Waller at his favourite place, the piano.

Top: Looking quite the dandy.

Left: Fats poses with the Creole Dancing Revue, Culver City, California, 1935.

Hank Williams

KING OF COUNTRY
17 SEPTEMBER 1923 – I JANUARY 1953

Hank Williams became a country legend with self-penned songs about love and loss. His lyrics were a reflection of a troubled private life, which he dealt with by consuming alcohol and drugs.

developed a taste for liquor, in part to numb the pain of a congenital spinal defect. He later became hooked on painkillers.

In 1944 Hank married farm girl Audrey Mae Sheppard, who encouraged him to raise his sights. Williams signed a publishing deal in 1946 and began recording on the minor Sterling label. A year later,

'You got to have smelt a lot of mule manure before you can sing like a hillbilly.'

Born Hiram Williams in Mount Olive, Alabama, Williams was given a guitar when he was seven. Hank picked up the rudiments of the instrument from a black street musician who went by the name Tee-Tot. That grounding gave his music a blues infusion, his lyrics an air of plaintive melancholy.

The family relocated to Montgomery when Hank was 14. He won talent contests, formed a band called The Drifting Cowboys and was dubbed 'The Singing Kid' on local radio. There was also a long apprenticeship on the bar-room circuit, where fights broke out routinely. Hank

Above: Hank Williams plays with the Drifting Cowboys.

Right: Williams and his wife Audrey, circa 1950.

Opposite: A publicity portrait shows the young Williams.

he was on the MGM Records roster, debuting with 'Move It On Over'. He received a rapturous reception when he took his first bow at the Grand Ole Opry in 1949, the year in which 'Lovesick Blues' was a fixture in the charts. 'Cold Cold Heart', 'Why Don't You Love Me' and 'Hey Good Lookin'' were among a slew of Country chart-toppers, but Williams's songs had wide enough appeal to feature in the *Billboard* Hot 100. Ray Charles, The Carpenters and Tony Bennett were among the many artists who had hits with covers of his songs.

In 1952, three years after the birth of future Country star Hank Jr, the Williams's marriage hit the buffers. Hank's wayward behaviour made him *persona non grata* in Nashville, and there were unpleasant scenes when he appeared on stage the worse for wear. A whirlwind marriage in October 1952 couldn't halt the self-destructive slide. Reduced to playing lesser venues, Williams had an important concert booking in Canton, Ohio, scheduled for New Year's Day 1953. He suffered heart failure en route, expiring in the back of his chauffeur-driven Cadillac. His final single, 'I'll Never Get Out of this World Alive', went to No 1, the first of several posthumous reissues that saw him top the charts for six months that year.

Princess Diana Tony Han
Amy John
Jackson Pollock Alexander
Amelia Earhart

Also Leaving the Stage

Lenny Bruce

CONTROVERSIAL COMIC
13 OCTOBER 1925 – 3 AUGUST 1966

As a satirist and iconoclast, Lenny Bruce targeted many sacred cows. The Establishment, in turn, trained its sights on a comedian whose humour was based on 'destruction and despair'.

Satire, said Lenny Bruce, could be defined as 'tragedy plus time'. Just a few short years after his death, Bruce's routines could be delivered without fear of rebuke or censure. But in the early 1960s his singular brand of envelope-pushing landed him in plenty of hot water, and the battles with the authorities – even those he won – exacted a heavy toll.

A New Yorker born Leonard Alfred Schneider, Bruce drifted from job to job after leaving the US Navy in 1946, before finding his comedic niche on the club circuit. The quality of the venues improved after he won a TV talent show, and during the 1950s, with a failed marriage behind him, Bruce developed the no-holds-barred brand of stand-up, often improvised, that prompted admiration and outrage. His monologues on sex and organized religion were unflinchingly refreshing or nauseatingly obscene, according to taste ('Every day people are straying away from the church and going back to God'). He reviled cant and hypocrisy, railed against exploitation and prejudice. War, violence and racism were the real obscenities, not four-letter words or body parts. 'If something about the human body disgusts you,' he said, 'complain to the manufacturer.' In 'Psychopathia Sexualis' he tells of a man in love with a horse ('She looked so nice against the rail/With her pretty, long legs and ponytail.') Wickedly funny to some, beyond the pale to others.

> **'The only honest art form is laughter, comedy. You can't fake it.'**

He was arrested on obscenity charges in San Francisco in 1961, and although he was acquitted, it heralded the start of a long cat-and-mouse period of harassment. Nor was it confined to America. In 1962 the plug was pulled on his show in Australia, and a year

Left: Lenny Bruce performs at the Village Theater in Greenwich Village, New York, on 28 March 1964.

Opposite: Bruce looks introspective in the early 1960s.

later he was forbidden entry into Britain, where he was booked to appear at Peter Cook's Establishment Club in London.

When he wasn't attracting the authorities' attention with his material, Bruce brought them to his door for drugs possession. By the time he succumbed to a morphine overdose, the attritional battle had left him broke and virtually unemployable.

Lenny Bruce's willingness to tackle taboo subjects head-on paved the way for other sharp-edged comedians. He championed free speech and used the microphone to unsettle as well as entertain.

Diana,
Princess of Wales

THE PEOPLE'S PRINCESS
1 JULY 1961 – 31 AUGUST 1997

She was England's Rose, Queen of People's Hearts, the People's Princess. Diana, Princess of Wales was a dazzling beauty who enjoyed enormous privileges even before marrying into the royal family, yet she championed the cause of those less fortunate, her humanitarian and charity work earning her the admiration of people the world over. 'She reached out to people on the margins of society', as Nelson Mandela put it. Her own fairy-tale marriage unravelled, and she appeared on the verge of finding happiness when she died, as ever, with the paparazzi in close attendance.

Diana was the third of four children born to Earl Spencer – a former equerry to King George VI and Queen Elizabeth – and Frances Roche. She spent her childhood years at Park House on the Sandringham estate, her father inheriting the family seat at Althorp, Northamptonshire, when she was 13. By the mid-1970s her parents had divorced and both remarried. Diana was no academic high-flyer, self-deprecatingly describing herself as 'thick as a plank'. Her nurturing qualities were well to the fore, however, revealed in her easy manner with children and love of animals.

After completing her education, Diana took a job at the Young England kindergarten in Pimlico, London. Both her workplace and Kensington flat were besieged by journalists in the autumn of 1980, when rumours of a relationship with Prince Charles began to emerge. The future king had intimated that 30 was a good time to marry. He was 32, and the press pack scented a royal marriage in the air. Speculation ended with the

Left: Fairy-tale princess on her wedding day in 1981.

Above: The Prince and Princess of Wales with Princes William and Harry on a family holiday in 1987.

Opposite: Diana, one of the world's most glamorous and photographed women, pictured in 1985.

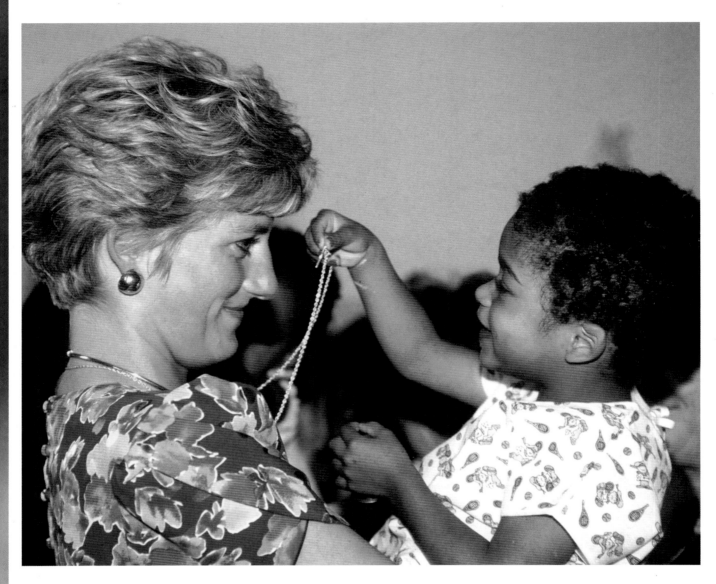

'I don't go by the rule book ... I lead from the heart, not the head.'

engagement announcement in February 1981, and the couple were married at St Paul's Cathedral on 29 July that year.

Diana had initially been dubbed 'shy Di' for the way she seemed to hide behind her curtain fringe as the photographers snapped away. She soon came into her own, her poise, charm, elegance and radiant beauty lighting up even the most workaday function. Twenty years after John F. Kennedy had been relegated to the role of 'the man who accompanied Jackie Kennedy to

Paris', here was a new consort who put the headline royal in the shade.

Prince William was born 11 months after the knot was tied, Prince Harry arriving in September 1985. Predictably, Diana was a demonstrative, hands-on mother, one who jealously guarded her parenting role and used nannies as sparingly as her busy schedule would allow. She took part in the mums' race at sports day and got a soaking on a water slide, and in doing so endeared herself all the more to the public. Here was a royal with the common touch. That reputation was enhanced by her willingness to extend a comforting hand to AIDS and leprosy sufferers. 'There are more important things in life than ballet,' said Diana, for whom dance was another passion. Even as she gave so much to the downtrodden and disadvantaged, her own life was in turmoil.

solace in the arms of ex-cavalry officer James Hewitt, and had to endure the airing of the 'Squidgygate' telephone conversations involving James Gilbey. The pressures had also taken a toll on her health as the gym fanatic was revealed to have battled bulimia. In December 1992 it was announced that she and Prince Charles were to separate; divorce proceedings were finalized in 1996.

One of the great fashion icons of the age raised millions for charity by auctioning off many of her outfits in 1997, and put the landmine issue on the front page after visiting Angola. That summer she also had a new man in her life. Her romance with Dodi Fayed brought fleeting happiness before both were killed in a Parisian underpass as their car tried to outmanoeuvre the chasing paparazzi. The public outpouring was extraordinary. 'Show us you care' ran one headline, aimed at a royal family that appeared out of step with the national mood. The Queen responded with a personal address, describing Diana as 'an exceptional and gifted human being' who could 'inspire others with her warmth and kindness'. In his withering funeral speech the following day, Earl Spencer noted the irony that his sister, who had been given the name of the ancient goddess of hunting, was 'the most hunted person of the modern age'.

Opposite: Always eager to connect with with children, Diana holds a child during a visit to a hostel for abandoned children, many of whom are HIV positive, in São Paolo, Brazil, in 1997.

Above: The princess chats to an Angolan landmine victim and (right) on a visit to an area cleared of landmines, Angola, 1997.

By the mid-1980s the marriage was in trouble, and over time the frostiness between the Waleses became all too evident. The image of Diana sitting alone in front of the Taj Mahal – a monument to grand passion – captured the sense of isolation she had felt for years. It was taken during a visit to India in 1992, the year in which Andrew Morton's book *Diana: Her True Story* revealed the hollowness of the union. Prince Charles had been in a long-term clandestine relationship with Camilla Parker Bowles, reviving a romance that had begun prior to her marriage in 1973. Diana sought

Amelia Earhart

PIONEERING AVIATRIX
24 JULY 1898 – 2 JULY 1937

Amelia Earhart's aeronautical exploits captured the public imagination at a time when flying was a high-risk, seat-of-the-pants endeavour. Her solo crossing of the Atlantic in 1932 was one of many record-breaking achievements, and it was while undertaking yet another daredevil adventure five years later that she met her end.

The inter-war years have been called a golden age for aviation, an era before jet propulsion and airliners with hotel-style creature comforts. Air travel was exotic and romantic. Those who took to the skies were fêted for the intrepid, insouciant manner in which they carried out their gravity-defying feats; doubly so when women got in on an act that had been something of a male preserve in its short history. Amelia Earhart was in the vanguard, showing that gender was irrelevant. She would take her place alongside the Wright brothers, Louis Blériot, Alcock and Brown and Charles Lindbergh as one of aviation's valiant pioneers, one who forfeited her life trying to push back yet another boundary.

Kansas-born Earhart's terrestrial occupations were prosaic. She worked as a nurse in a Canadian military hospital during World War I, then set down in Boston, where she trained as a social worker. Tomboyish in childhood, Earhart carried her feisty, adventurous spirit into adult life. She took a particular interest in women who had succeeded in male-dominated environments, and it was one such area that completely captivated her after she took her first flight in 1920.

In the aftermath of the global conflict there was a glut of decommissioned planes around and an aspiring pilot could get airborne for a few hundred dollars. There were also numerous records up for grabs. It wasn't long before she had her second-hand biplane up to 14,000 feet, the first of many record-breaking ventures.

Earhart came to the world's attention in June 1928, when she became the first woman to fly across the Atlantic. She was by now an experienced pilot, but took

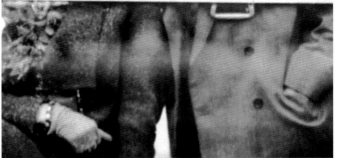

Top: Amelia Earhart and her husband, publisher George Palmer Putnam, laughing and looking out a window while travelling by train in Cherbourg, France, June 1932.

Right: L–R: American First Lady Eleanor Roosevelt, aviator Amelia Earhart, Jim and Amy Mollison (formerly Amy Johnson) and President Roosevelt, New York, 1933.

Opposite: Amelia Earhart pictured in 1932.

a back seat on this trip as she was not proficient in flying by instruments. Bill Stultz was at the controls of the triple-engine Fokker seaplane for the 20 hours 40 minutes it took to get from Newfoundland to Burry Port, south Wales. There was also a mechanic on board, but it was Earhart for whom the media and public clamoured. Though her role was a passive one, she took to the skies knowing that three women had recently perished undertaking the same journey. This milestone crossing and other achievements earned her the tag 'Lady Lindy', for she bore a passing likeness to compatriot Charles Lindbergh, who had made his own celebrated transatlantic flight the previous year.

In 1931 Earhart married publisher and publicist George Putnam, who had been heavily involved in the

1928 venture. He helped mastermind the trip for which she is best known: emulating Lindbergh to become the first woman to fly solo across the Atlantic. It took place, quite deliberately, on the fifth anniversary of Lindbergh's flight: 20 May 1932. She opted for a fast, single-engine Lockheed Vega, which carried her from Newfoundland to Londonderry in 14 hours 56 minutes, also a record. On her return home Congress awarded her the Distinguished Flying Cross, making her the first female recipient of that award.

Before the year was out she had set a new mark by flying solo across America, from Los Angeles to New Jersey. There was also a long-standing altitude record for autogiros, while in January 1935 Earhart completed the first solo flight from Hawaii to California, a 2,400-mile trip that had claimed several lives. There was little left for her to accomplish, save for a circumnavigation of the globe, and this was what she planned as she approached her 40th birthday.

What was to have been the crowning glory of her flying career got off to an inauspicious start as Earhart pranged her Lockheed Electra while taking off from Hawaii, having departed from Oakland, California. After repairs were made, Earhart and her navigator, Fred Noonan, set off for the second time on 1 June 1937, this time taking a west–east route. Everything proceeded according to plan, the finishing line almost in view when disaster struck. Having reached New Guinea, Earhart's next destination was Howland Island in the middle of the Pacific Ocean. It was a 2,500-mile leg, the outer limit of the plane's range, and there was no margin for error in finding what was a tiny speck of land. The final radio message said that fuel was reaching a critical level and land had still not been sighted. An exhaustive search of the area was carried out, the US Government

'**Obviously I faced the possibility of not returning when first I considered going. Once faced and settled, there really wasn't any good reason to refer to it.**'

expending millions of dollars in the hope that one of the country's most celebrated adventurers had managed to ditch safely. Neither the bodies nor the wreckage were recovered. Amelia Earhart disappeared on 2 July 1937 and was declared legally dead in January 1939.

Opposite: Amelia Earhart arrives in Southampton after piloting her plane, Friendship, from Burry Port, Wales.

Below: Earhart arrives in Los Angeles from Honolulu, where she crashed during her attempted flight around the world in 1937. With her are Harry Manning (left) and Fred Noonan.

Anne Frank

VOICE OF A LOST GENERATION
12 JUNE 1929 – MARCH 1945

Anne Frank and her family spent two years hiding in a 'secret annexe' in Amsterdam during the World War II. Her diary records the hopes and fears of an adolescent girl, the daily struggle to survive when discovery was a constant threat. It stands as a testament to the indomitable nature of the human spirit.

Annelies Marie Frank was born in Frankfurt to a prosperous Jewish family. Anne and her older sister Margot's comfortable upbringing was disturbed by the rise of the National Socialists, who were agitating against the country's Jewish population long before Hitler became Chancellor in 1933. Anti-Semitism then became part of the state machinery, and the Franks knew it was time to leave.

Otto Frank set up in business in Amsterdam, which became the family's new home, but the Franks's world was disrupted again in May 1940, when the Netherlands fell to the German Army. In July 1942 Anne's father implemented his plan to save the family from deportation: along with four Dutch Jews, the Frank family hid in part of Otto's business premises at 263 Prinsengracht. A bookcase covered the entrance to their attic quarters and their lifeline to the outside world was a small group of business colleagues and friends, who risked their own lives by bringing essential supplies. During office hours, when the premises were in use, it was especially important for Anne and the others to conduct themselves in near silence. Anne spent a lot of her time reading and writing, the latter including fictional tales as well as keeping her diary up to date.

Four months later, on 4 August 1944, the Gestapo discovered the hiding place after receiving an anonymous tip-off. The Franks were sent to Auschwitz, where Anne's mother died in January 1945. Anne and her sister were moved on to Bergen-Belsen

'I feel the suffering of millions. And yet, when I look up at the sky, I somehow feel that everything will change for the better, that this cruelty too shall end, that peace and tranquillity will return once more.'

concentration camp. Both succumbed to typhus a matter of weeks before the liberating forces arrived.

Anne's diary was found by one of the group who had helped sustain them during their 25-month ordeal. Otto Frank took possession, and after some hesitation decided to fulfil Anne's dream of seeing *The Secret Annexe* on the bookshelves, spreading its uplifting message and in the process preserving her memory. The diary became a publishing phenomenon, adapted for both stage and screen. It remains a powerful personal record of a teenage girl's awakening during one of the darkest chapters in human history.

Opposite: A portrait of Anne Frank taken in May 1942.

Above: The interior of Anne Frank's bedroom in the Anne Frank House Museum, Amsterdam, and the exterior of the house on Prinsengracht (Top).

Yuri Gagarin

FIRST MAN IN SPACE
9 MARCH 1934 – 27 MARCH 1968

On 12 April 1961, Soviet Russia beat the USA in the space race by becoming the first nation to successfully send a human into outer space. Yuri Gagarin, Soviet pilot and cosmonaut, left Earth at 9:07 local time and completed an orbit of the Earth, returning just 108 minutes later.

Yuri Alekseyevich Gagarin was born in a small village near the town of Gzhatsk – which was later renamed Gagarin. He was interested in flying and outer space from an early age and became a pilot in the Soviet Air Force, rising to the rank of lieutenant. In 1960 he was chosen as one of the candidates for the Soviet space programme and entered an elite training course to test his physical

and mental endurance. In 1961, after seven test flights – several of them failures – scientists decided the *Vostok* spacecraft was ready to carry a human passenger and Gagarin was selected from 20 young pilots on the short list. Apart from his outstanding performance in training tests, another factor in his favour was his size; the *Vostok*'s cabin was tiny and Gagarin was only 5 ft 2 inches tall.

'I could have gone on flying through space for ever.'

There were considerable concerns about the effect of weightlessness on a human; scientists worried Gagarin might pass out or go mad, so he was not expected to fly the craft, which was all automatic. A few things did go wrong: an antenna malfunction had put the *Vostok* into a much higher and riskier orbit, on re-entry a fault in a retrorocket made the ship rotate swiftly, and the landing capsule was slow to jettison the service module. However, Gagarin managed to bail out as planned and parachuted safely into a field outside Moscow, terrifying locals with his bright orange suit and space helmet.

After his historic flight Gagarin was awarded Hero of the Soviet Union, Soviet Russia's highest honour, and became an international celebrity, demonstrating a talent for being in the public eye and charming

Below: Yuri Gagarin strapped into position aboard the Vostok *spaceship in 1961.*

Top: Gagarin with first woman cosmonaut, Valentina Tereshkova, in 1963.

Opposite: Gagarin speaks surrounded by well-wishers in 1962.

everyone with his cheerful smile. He later became deputy training director of the Cosmonaut Training Centre outside Moscow, which was eventually named after him. He died on a routine training flight when a MiG 15 jet he was piloting crashed. Investigators concluded the plane had either swerved sharply to avoid something and gone into an uncontrollable spin, or that a cabin air vent had been left open, causing oxygen deprivation to the crew so they were unable to control the aircraft.

Tony Hancock

'THE LAD HIMSELF'
12 MAY 1924 – 24/25 JUNE 1968

Tony Hancock was the archetypal sad clown, a comedy genius riddled with insecurity and self-doubt. His long-running TV series made him one Britain's best-loved entertainers of the postwar era, and set the benchmark for the sitcom genre.

Having spent the first three years of his life in Birmingham, Tony Hancock and family headed south to Bournemouth, where his father combined running a hotel with fulfilling his show-business ambitions. As a schoolboy Tony set his sights on a stage career, and comedy was his chosen vehicle. He got his break during World War II, performing on the army-camp circuit. His material was somewhat risqué, but after one salutary experience at a church hall, where his near-the-knuckle jokes fell flat, Hancock quite literally resolved to clean up his act.

Throughout the 1940s and early 50s Hancock honed his craft in variety shows and on radio, but the major turning point came in 1954, when *Hancock's Half Hour* first hit the airwaves. It ran until 1959, by which time it had transferred successfully to television, the two enormously popular shows running in tandem for three years. Billed as 'the lad himself', he was twice voted the country's top comedian, and at its height the TV show attracted audiences of 20 million.

Both shows were written by Alan Galton and Ray Simpson, whose scripts gave us a window into the world of Anthony Aloysius St John Hancock, the pompous, pretentious, opinionated occupant of 23 Railway Cuttings, East Cheam. His trademarks were a homburg, astrakhan-collared coat and exasperated 'Stone me!' as he launched into his latest tirade. Everyday situations prompted Hancock to hold forth: being stuck in a lift, giving blood, a library visit, jury service, a broken TV set.

'I play up pretensions, pomposity and stupidity in order, I hope, to destroy them.'

Below: Hancock and Sid James rehearse the 'Missing Page' episode of Hancock's Half Hour *in 1960.*

Top: With Freddie Ross on their wedding day in 1965.

Opposite: The lad himself photographed in 1965.

Hancock was popular in Commonwealth countries but failed to crack America. He starred in two films, *The Rebel* (1960) and *The Punch and Judy Man* (1962). By the time he made the latter he had discarded Galton and Simpson, and it showed. Indeed, he ditched many of those who helped make his show an institution. His self-destructive side came to the fore as decline set in, heavy drinking impacting on both his personal and professional life. Hancock took a fatal overdose while trying to relaunch his career in Australia, leaving a suicide note that read: 'Things seemed to go too wrong too many times.'

Keith Haring

STREET ARTIST
4 MAY 1958 – 16 FEBRUARY 1990

Artist and social activist Keith Haring developed a pared-down style to express universal concepts of birth, death, love, sex and war. His work was inspired by street culture and during his short, intense career he participated in over 100 exhibitions and was featured in countless magazine articles.

Haring was born in Pennsylvania, the oldest of four children, and started to draw after learning basic cartooning skills from his father. After high school he attended art school in Pittsburgh, but left after less than a year; he continued to study and work independently and had his first solo exhibition at only 19. In 1978 he moved to New York and enrolled in the School of Visual Arts, but quickly became involved in an alternative art

'My contribution to the world is my ability to draw.'

community thriving alongside the established museum and gallery circuit. It was here that Haring found his style in simple line artworks – and, inspired by the public nature of Christo's work and Warhol's fusion of art and life, he also began to devote his career to creating art for a wider audience.

In 1980 Haring found the ideal place to experiment: in the subway, empty advertising panels were covered in matte black paper that was ideal for chalk drawings. In the following five years he created hundreds of 'subway drawings' and commuters often stopped to speak to him as he worked, providing valuable feedback. He soon became widely known, with his work featured in magazines and newspapers and solo shows at several

Left: Haring works on the wall of a Paris Métro station in 1984.

Above: Andy Warhol and Keith Haring in 1986.

Opposite: Haring in his studio, circa 1980.

galleries. For his first show in New York he painted all the walls with his art, then displayed his paintings and sculptures. Haring soon began to travel around the world, with shows in Europe, Japan and across the USA. His work became very expensive, but since he still wanted it to be accessible to everyone he opened the Pop Shop to sell his art on posters, badges, T-shirts and games.

Despite his growing fame, Haring was still committed to public art, creating artworks for charities, hospitals and children's centres around the world. He also worked with students in schools to paint large murals, ran workshops for children and created artwork for public-service campaigns. In 1988 he was diagnosed with AIDS and the following year established the Keith Haring Foundation to provide funding and artworks for AIDS organizations and children's programmes. He died of AIDS-related complications, having spent the last years of his life working to raise awareness of the illness.

241

Steve Irwin

CROCODILE HUNTER AND CONSERVATIONIST
22 FEBRUARY 1962 – 4 SEPTEMBER 2006

A decade after *Crocodile Dundee* hit the cinema screens, Steve Irwin became a household name as a real-life outback adventurer who enthused people with his passion for animals. A brush with a fearsome saltwater crocodile or Komodo dragon might elicit a trademark 'Crikey!' but this bluff, breezy, larger-than-life character was only ever stirred to protect them, never shaken.

Irwin's family home was a menagerie, to which was added a python in 1968, a gift for his sixth birthday. His parents were committed naturalists who in 1970 gave up their day jobs and relocated to Queensland, where they founded Beerwah Reptile Park. His father began capturing and relocating 'problem' crocodiles under a state-sponsored programme, and Steve, who captured his first croc before his tenth birthday, spent the 1980s carrying on this work and helping run the renamed Queensland Reptile and Fauna Park. When he began making TV documentaries in the 1990s, it didn't take long to come up with a snappy title: *The Crocodile Hunter*. He presented the *The Ten Deadliest Snakes in the World*, and even starred in the 2002 movie *The Crocodile Hunter: Collision Course*. Irwin had an uncanny rapport with wildlife, once relating how he approached a pride of lions, animals he had never worked with before. Success meant there was the occasional glitzy awards ceremony to attend – he was nominated for an Emmy in 2000 – but Irwin preferred his khaki work clothes to dinner suits. In 1991 he took over the running of the family wildlife park, later

> ## 'I have no fear of losing my life – if I have to save a koala or a crocodile or a kangaroo or a snake, mate, I will save it.'

renamed Australia Zoo. The following year he married American conservationist Terri Raines, a kindred spirit whose speciality in her home state of Oregon had been cougars. Their honeymoon was spent tracking crocodiles, and as soon as daughter Bindi and son Robert were born, they, too, were introduced to the animals their parents dealt with on a daily basis. That created a media storm in 2004, when Irwin was criticized for feeding a crocodile while holding his infant son.

He died two years later in a freak accident, a stingray barb puncturing his chest while he was filming on the Great Barrier Reef. Australia's prime minister John Howard said the country had lost 'a wonderful and colourful son'. The name of this great naturalist, educator and showman lives on in *Steve's Whale One*, an excursion vessel that was one of his long-cherished dreams, and in the Steve Irwin Wildlife Reserve in Cape York, Queensland.

Opposite, top and right: Steve Irwin pictured at Australia Zoo doing what he enjoyed most.

Amy Johnson

'QUEEN OF THE AIR'
1 JULY 1903 – 5 JANUARY 1941

Amy Johnson broke down gender barriers with her intrepid achievements in a male-dominated field. Her aeronautical feats inspired a popular song, elevated her into a role model and made her a national heroine.

Amy Johnson was a spirited, adventurous individual who was never going to be fulfilled by the secretarial work she took up after leaving university. The five-shilling flight she took in 1926 was more to her liking, though it would be three years before she obtained her pilot's licence. Johnson also became one of the first women to hold an Air Ministry ground engineer's licence, proving that she had maintenance skills to match her flying capabilities. From the outset she was determined to make aviation her career. 'I'll fly till I die,' she said, 'and I hope I die flying.'

> '*Had I been a man, I might have explored the Poles or climbed Mount Everest, but as it was, my spirit found an outlet in the air.*'

Johnson became an instant celebrity with her solo flight from Britain to Australia in May 1930. The 19-day journey wasn't quite enough to establish a record, but she was the first woman to complete such an undertaking. Stories about the eventful trip in the second-hand, open-cockpit Gipsy Moth she called *Jason* filled newspaper columns and made Johnson a media darling. Dubbed 'Queen of the Air', she received £10,000 from one national daily, and gained the royal

Top: Amy Johnson pictured with her Gipsy Moth just before embarking on a solo flight to Australia, 5 May 1930.

Left: Johnson celebrates breaking the record for a flight between London and Cape Town, 1932.

Opposite: A portrait dating from the late 1930s.

seal of approval when she was made a Commander of the Order of the British Empire.

More epic trips followed, Johnson bagging a number of records along the way. She flew solo to Japan in 1931, and a year later clipped ten hours off the London–Cape Town record, making the trip in four days and seven hours. The man whose time she had bettered was her new husband James Mollison, a renowned aviator in his own right. Theirs would be a troubled marriage, chiefly down to Mollison's philandering and bibulousness, but before they divorced in 1938 the couple undertook several joint enterprises. In 1933 they received a tickertape reception in New York after completing a 39-hour transatlantic flight, though they did crash-land in Bridgeport, Connecticut, after running out of fuel. The following year saw them make a non-stop trip to India in record time.

Soon after war broke out, Johnson joined the Air Transport Auxiliary, flying aircraft from factories to RAF bases. It was during one of these ferrying trips that her plane went down in the Thames Estuary. One eyewitness account said Johnson baled out, but her body was never recovered and she was presumed drowned.

Frida Kahlo

FEMINIST SURREALIST
6 JULY 1907 – 13 JULY 1954

Magdalena Carmen Frieda Kahlo y Calderón is perhaps best known for her self-portraits; her paintings are also remembered for their intense, vibrant colours. In Mexico her work is celebrated for its basis in national folk art, and it is also well regarded by feminists for its uncompromising depiction of the female form.

'I never paint dreams or nightmares. I paint my own reality.'

At 22 Kahlo married the famous Mexican muralist Diego Rivera, who was 20 years her senior. Their stormy, passionate relationship survived infidelities on both sides, the pressures of their careers, Kahlo's bisexuality, her continuing poor health and her inability to have children. When Kahlo discovered Rivera had had an affair with her younger sister they did briefly divorce, but remarried again the following year. Both Kahlo and Rivera were very active in the Communist Party

Left: Kahlo and Rivera work in a studio. Kahlo's self-portrait, 'The Two Fridas' (1939), hangs in the background.

Below: Kahlo, her husband and a pet monkey pictured in 1944.

Opposite: A portrait dating from circa 1940.

Kahlo was born in Mexico City and at six she contracted polio; although she survived, one leg was permanently wasted. When she was 18, she was seriously injured in a bus accident, suffering fractures to her spine, collarbone and ribs, a shattered pelvis, shoulder and foot injuries, and damage that later prevented her from having children. She spent over a year confined to bed and during her convalescence began to paint. Her paintings, mostly self-portraits and still lifes, were deliberately naïve, filled with the colours and forms of Mexico and often featuring the suggestion of physical or psychological pain.

and they were on good terms with Leon Trotsky when he first arrived in Mexico after fleeing Stalin's regime. In early July 1954, Kahlo made her last public appearance, when she participated in a Communist demonstration.

During her lifetime Kahlo's paintings were not widely known, although the Louvre in Paris had bought one of her paintings in 1939. However, 30 years after she died a retrospective of her work was shown in Europe as well as in New York and Mexico City; several books about her were also published and a film of her life was released. Since then there has been an increasing interest in and respect for her work.

In her last year Kahlo suffered from declining health and one leg had to be amputated due to gangrene, which was a devastating blow to her self-esteem. She officially died from a pulmonary embolism, but a few people thought that she may have found a way to commit suicide. Her last diary entry read: 'I hope the end is joyful – and I hope never to come back. Frida.'

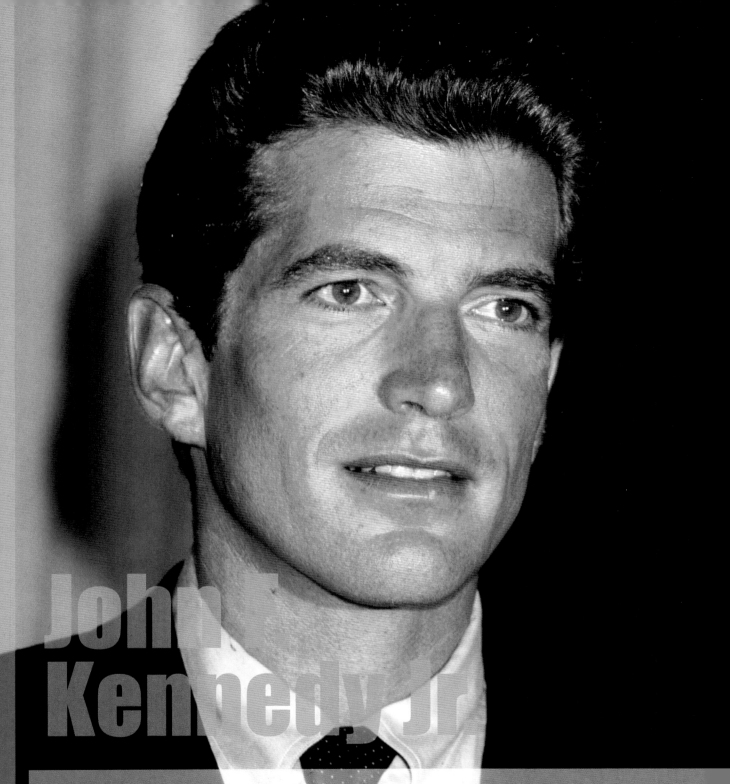

AMERICAN ROYALTY
25 NOVEMBER 1960 – 16 JULY 1999

John F. Kennedy Jr lived his whole life in the spotlight. Born only weeks after his charismatic father was elected president, he was the first infant to live in the White House since the Cleveland administration. But tragedy struck early, and on his third birthday, he was watched by grieving millions across the world when he stepped forward and saluted the coffin at his father's funeral.

Seeking privacy, Jackie Kennedy moved her family to New York and following the assassination of Bobby Kennedy and her marriage to Aristotle Onassis, her priority was to protect her children from both danger and the glare of the media. John Jr went from the elite Phillips Academy in Andover to Brown University, graduating in 1983. Although he apparently wanted to become an actor, he followed his mother's wishes and enrolled in New York University's Law School; he failed the bar exam twice, before passing, temporarily earning the nickname 'the hunk who flunked'.

In 1988 John Jr introduced his uncle, Senator Edward M. Kennedy, at the Democratic Convention, prompting speculation that he was preparing to run for office himself. Instead he went to work as a prosecutor for the Manhattan District Attorney; in his short but successful career he never lost a case. In 1995 he began a career in publishing by launching *George* magazine, a glossy journal that aimed to cover wider political issues in an impartial and entertaining way. John Jr not only edited the magazine, but also wrote essays and conducted interviews – even criticizing his own Kennedy relatives on occasion.

Handsome, charming and polite, John Jr was dubbed 'sexiest man alive' at one point and he dated

Top: John Jr pictured with his mother in 1989.

Right: John Jr with his wife Carolyn Bessette in 1999.

Opposite: Kennedy attends a press conference to launch George magazine, 1995.

'It's hard for me to talk about a legacy or a mystique... we're a family like any other.'

several movie stars. However, in 1996 he married Carolyn Bessette, a former Calvin Klein executive. A keen sportsman, John Jr was often seen skating around his neighbourhood or jogging in Central Park. He also loved flying, and in July 1999 he took off to pilot a small plane to Martha's Vineyard, with his wife and her sister as passengers. He had just had an ankle cast removed after a crash in a paraglider three weeks earlier, and was still limping – this was the first time he was able to fly solo since the accident. The three never arrived; the plane crashed into the ocean near its destination, apparently due to pilot error.

Alexander
McQueen

BAD BOY OF FASHION
17 MARCH 1969 – 11 FEBRUARY 2010

Born in the East End of London, the son of a taxi driver, Lee Alexander McQueen was the quintessential bad boy made good, eventually being honoured with a CBE from Queen Elizabeth II for services to the fashion industry.

McQueen left school at 16 to train with Savile Row tailors Anderson & Sheppard and then Gieves & Hawkes, but later won a coveted place at London's Central Saint Martins College of Art and Design to do a master's degree in fashion design. Influential stylist Isabella Blow bought his entire 1991 degree

show; after her suicide in 2007 he dedicated his Spring/Summer 2008 collection to her memory.

In 1996 McQueen became John Galliano's successor at Givenchy and, although he said himself that his first collection for the label was 'crap', he stayed until 2001, creating a series of challenging and eye-catching collections. His provocative designs often led to controversy and criticism, but during this period he received the British Designer of the Year award three times. However, when his contract with Givenchy ended in 2001 McQueen was glad to escape, saying that it had 'constrained his creativity'. He began a new company, Alexander McQueen, with the Gucci Group holding a majority shareholding and McQueen himself as creative director. His designs combined masterful tailoring and haute couture sensibility with an imagination that ran from the obscure to the sublime; models were sent down the catwalk in 12-inch platform heels, with their hair teased into horns or dressed in amphibian-like breastplates. The shows themselves were renowned for their mix of surreal vision and elaborate and theatrical accessories, and quickly became the highlight of Paris Fashion Week. In 2003 McQueen not only won the British Designer of the Year award for a fourth time, but was also named International Fashion Designer of the Year.

'When you see a woman in my clothes, you want to know more about them.'

By 2008 Alexander McQueen was a fashion empire with stores across the world; countless celebrities adored McQueen's designs and were regularly photographed wearing them. Openly gay, McQueen once described himself as the 'pink sheep of the family'. He briefly 'married' film-maker George Forsyth and although the couple later parted they remained friends. Throughout his life McQueen was very close to his mother and he was devastated when she died in February 2010. Nine days later, the day before her funeral, he was found hanging in his London flat, having slashed his wrists and taken a huge overdose of cocaine and sleeping pills.

Top: Alexander McQueen on the catwalk at the end of a show, Paris, 2004.

Right: Sarah Jessica Parker and McQueen at the Metropolitan Museum of Art, New York, 2006.

Opposite: McQueen seen during London Fashion Week, 2006.

Jackson Pollock

ABSTRACT EXPRESSIONIST
28 JANUARY 1912 – 11 AUGUST 1956

Jackson Pollock's name is associated with a style of painting that avoids any points of emphasis or identifiable parts and abandons the traditional ideas of composition. The abstract images often had no relation to the shape or size of the canvas – sometimes in the finished work the canvas was trimmed to suit the contents.

Paul Jackson Pollock was born in Cody, Wyoming, and began to study painting in 1929 at the Art Students' League, New York, under Thomas Hart Benton, an artist known for his depiction of rural America – but also for his fluid use of colour and his fierce independence. During the 1930s Pollock was also influenced by Mexican muralist painter David Siqueiros, who first introduced him to the more experimental uses of liquid paint. From 1938 to 1942 Pollock worked for the Federal Art Project, which supported out-of-work artists by employing them to produce art for public buildings, such as schools, hospitals and libraries. In 1944 he married fellow artist Lee Krasner.

By the mid-1940s Pollock was painting in a completely abstract manner, and the 'drip and splash' style for which he is perhaps best known emerged with some abruptness in 1947. Instead of using a traditional easel he fixed his canvas to the floor or the wall and

'**My paintings do not have a centre, but depend on the same amount of interest throughout.**'

Left: Pollock drops sand onto a painting at his studio.

Above: Pollock and his wife Lee Krasner talk to a guest in 1949.

Opposite: Jackson Pollock in his studio, known as 'The Springs', East Hampton, New York, 1949.

poured, dripped, spattered or even flung paint from the can; instead of using brushes he manipulated the colour with sticks, trowels or knives, sometimes creating a heavy impasto with a mixture of sand, broken glass or other foreign matter. Rather than just standing relatively still and using a wrist action to paint, he moved around the canvas constantly, using his entire body to create. The theory was that this type of 'action painting' resulted in a direct expression or revelation of the unconscious moods of the artist. However, at the start of the 1950s Pollock abandoned the drip technique, although

he continued to produce paintings in the abstract expressionist style, as well as figurative or semi-figurative works and delicately modulated paintings in rich impasto.

Pollock had battled with alcoholism for many years and in 1956 he died at the wheel of his car, having crashed while driving under the influence. During his lifetime his style was so advanced that it was not widely understood, but by the 1960s he was generally recognized as the most important figure in the most important movement of the century in American painting.

Gianni Versace

MASTER OF STYLE
2 DECEMBER 1946 – 15 JULY 1997

The Versace style is a trademark of its own, known for its vivid colours, striking prints and impeccable construction. The collections, for both men and women, are often sexy almost to the point of vulgarity.

Gianni Versace was born in Reggio Calabria, Italy, where his mother owned a dressmaking shop. The young Versace learned the skills for making clothes early and was soon designing – his first dress, an off-the-shoulder gown in velvet, was made when he was only nine. Despite this he went on to study architecture, before choosing fashion as a career and moving to Milan when he was 25. His first chance to show his skills to a wider audience came in 1972, when he designed a collection for Fiori Fiorentini, a company based in Lucca. Soon he was designing for several Italian fashion houses, but the first time his own name was featured was in 1974, in a collection for Complice.

'My dream was always to be a composer, but fashion came very easily.'

By 1978 Versace had launched his own company with a womenswear collection under the label Gianni Versace Donna. He opened a signature boutique in Milan, although he still sold clothes from other labels as well. However, it was not long before the Versace style had become so popular that there were boutiques opening around the world. By 1979 he had begun

working with several well-known photographers, such as Richard Avedon – who became his favourite – Helmut Newton, Herb Ritts and Steven Meisel. In 1986 the first retrospectives of Versace's work were held in Chicago and Paris.

Versace was openly gay; he met his partner, Antonio D'Amico – a model – in 1982. They remained together until Versace's death, and were often seen out and about with celebrities such as Madonna and Elton John. Versace also became involved in the movie industry, designing costumes for films such as *Judge Dredd (1995) and A Life Less Ordinary* (1997). In addition he designed costumes for theatre, opera and ballet; he was awarded the very first American Fashion Oscar in 1993.

In 1997 Versace was shot by a spree killer outside his home in Miami, Florida, as he returned from an early morning stroll. His younger sister, Donatella – who had previously been his muse – became the new head of design, while older brother Santo became CEO of a fashion empire worth an estimated £500 million.

Above: Versace with supermodels (L–R) Karen Mulder, Linda Evangelista and Carla Bruni after a fashion show in Paris, 1995.

Top: Gianni Versace with his sister Donatella in 1996.

Opposite: Versace poses in LA in 1991.

Places to Visit
Some burial places & memorials

Music Makers: Pop & Rock

Marc Bolan: Golders Green Crematorium, London
Karen Carpenter: Pierce Brothers Valley Oaks Memorial Park, Los Angeles
Ian Curtis: Macclesfield Cemetery, UK
Nick Drake: St Mary Magdalene Churchyard, Tanworth-in-Arden, UK
Cass Elliot: Mount Sinai Memorial Park, Los Angeles
Andy Gibb: Forest Lawns, Hollywood Hills, Los Angeles
Jimi Hendrix: Greenwood Memorial Park, Renton, Washington
Buddy Holly: City of Lubbock Cemetery, Lubbock, Texas
Michael Jackson: Forest Lawns, Hollywood Hills, Los Angeles
Brian Jones: Cheltenham Cemetery, UK
John Lennon: Strawberry Fields, Central Park, New York
Bob Marley: Bob Marley Mausoleum, St Ann, Jamaica
Jim Morrison: Père-Lachaise Cemetery, Paris
Elvis Presley: Graceland, Memphis, Tennessee
Ritchie Valens: San Fernando Mission Cemetery, Mission Hills, California
Frank Zappa: Westwood Memorial Park, Los Angeles

Politicians & Activists

Benazir Bhutto: Garhi Khuda Bakhsh, Sindh, Pakistan
Steve Biko: King Williams Town Cemetery, South Africa
Che Guevara: Villa Clara, Cuba
John F. Kennedy: Arlington National Cemetery, Washington, D.C.
Robert F. Kennedy: Arlington National Cemetery, Washington, D.C.
Martin Luther King Jr: Martin Luther King Jr National Historic Site, Atlanta, Georgia
Harvey Milk: San Francisco Columbarium, California
Eva Perón: La Recoleta Cemetery, Buenos Aires, Argentina
Malcolm X: Ferncliff Cemetery, Hartsdale, New York

Actors

John Belushi: Abel's Hill Cemetery, Martha's Vineyard Massachusetts
John Candy: Holy Cross Cemetery, Culver City, California
Montgomery Clift: The Quaker Friends Cemetery, Brooklyn, New York
James Dean: Park Cemetery, Fairmount, Indiana
Rainer Werner Fassbinder: Bogenhausener Friedhof, Munich, Germany
Judy Garland: Ferncliff Cemetery, Hartsdale, New York
Jean Harlow: Forest Lawn, Glendale, California
Grace Kelly: Cathedral of St Nicholas, Monte Carlo
Heath Ledger: Karrakatta Cemetery, Perth, Australia
Bruce Lee: Lakeview Cemetery, Seattle, Washington
Marilyn Monroe: Westwood Memorial Park, Los Angeles
John Ritter: Forest Lawns, Hollywood Hills, California
Romy Schneider: Boissy-sans-Avoir, Île de France, France

Sharon Tate: Holy Cross Cemetery, Culver City, Los Angeles
Rudolph Valentino: Hollywood Forever, Los Angeles
Natalie Wood: Westwood Memorial Park, Los Angeles

Sports Stars

Arthur Ashe: Woodland Cemetery, Richmond City, Virginia
Seve Ballesteros: Pedreña, Spain
Maureen Connolly: Sparkman Hillcrest Memorial Park, Texas
Duncan Edwards: Dudley Cemetery, UK
Lou Gehrig: Kensico Cemetery, Valhalla, New York
Bruce McLaren: Waikumete Cemetery, Auckland, New Zealand
Thurman Munson: Sunset Hills Memory Gardens, Canton, Ohio
Ayrton Senna: Morumbi Cemetery, São Paulo, Brazil
Payne Stewart: Doctor Phillips Cemetery, Orlando, Florida

Music Makers: Jazz, Classical & Country Music

Bix Beiderbecke: Oakdale Memorial Gardens, Davenport, Iowa
Jacques Brel: Atuona Cemetery, Atuona, French Polynesia
Maria Callas: Père-Lachaise Cemetery, Paris
Patsy Cline: Shenandoah Memorial Park, Winchester, Virginia
Nat King Cole: Forest Lawn Cemetery, Glendale, California
John Coltrane: Pinelake Memorial Park, Farmingdale, New York
Sam Cooke: Forest Lawn Cemetery, Glendale, California
Jacqueline du Pré: Golders Green Jewish Cemetery, London
George Gershwin: Westchester Cemetery, Hastings-on-Hudson, New York
Billie Holiday: New St Raymonds Cemetery, Bronx, New York
Mario Lanza: Holy Cross Cemetery, Culver City, California
Charlie Parker: Lincoln Cemetery, Kansas City, Missouri
Édith Piaf: Père-Lachaise Cemetery, Paris
Bessie Smith: Mount Lawn Cemetery, Sharon Hill, Pennsylvania
Hank Williams: Oakwood Annex Cemetery, Montgomery, Alabama

Also Leaving the Stage

Lenny Bruce: Eden Memorial Park, Mission Hills, California
Diana, Princess of Wales: Althorp, Northamptonshire, UK
Amelia Earhart: International Forest of Friendship, Atchison, Kansas
Anne Frank: Bergen-Belsen, Germany; Anne Frank House, Amsterdam
Yuri Gagarin: Ashes placed in the Kremlin Wall, Moscow
Tony Hancock: St Dunstan churchyard, Cranford, London
Steve Irwin: Australia Zoo, Beerwah, Queensland, Australia
Frida Kahlo: La Casa Azul (museum), Mexico City, Mexico
Jackson Pollock: Green River Cemetery, East Hampton, New York
Gianni Versace: Moltrasion Cemetery, Como, Italy